This Wasn't Supposed to Happen

Susan Crain Bakos

THIS WASN'T SUPPOSED TO HAPPEN

Single Women Over 30
Talk Frankly
About Their Lives

CONTINUUM ◆ NEW YORK

1985
The Continuum Publishing Company
370 Lexington Avenue, New York, N.Y. 10017

Library of Congress Cataloging in Publication Data

Bakos, Susan Crain.
  This wasn't supposed to happen.

  1. Single women—United States. 2. Divorced
women—United States. 3. Single women—United States—
Attitudes. 4. Divorced women—United States—Attitudes.
I. Title.
HQ800.4.U6B35 1985   305.4'890652   85-9659
ISBN 0-8264-0360-3

For my son, Richard,
and my niece, Julie Jirauch
—two children of
single women over thirty

Contents

Acknowledgments

This book could not have been written without the encouragement and support of the following people:

Jack Heidenry, my editor at Continuum, who pushed me when I needed a push;

Merry Clark and Jim Head, my editors at King Features Syndicate, who first suggested the stories of single women over thirty should be told;

John Peecher, my partner and friend, who read and reacted to each chapter and held my hand as needed;

Susan Lucco and the staff of the Edwardsville Public Library, who provided research direction for this book and so many other projects.

I also owe a special debt to the people (past and present) at *St. Louis* magazine, who have believed in me and helped me grow as a writer during the eight years of our association: Jack and Pat Heidenry, my first editors; Libby Ferguson, the publisher; and Michaele Gold, currently executive editor; and a debt of a different kind to Ruth and Erwin Brinkmann for patience and understanding.

And I am grateful to the single women who told me their stories, not all of which appear in these pages. The women who are here have consented to share their lives completely with us. To protect their privacy, I have given them different names—and in some cases changed the names of the cities in which they live or their professions.

This Wasn't Supposed to Happen

This Wasn't Supposed to Happen

*Will you, won't you, will you, won't you, will you join
the dance?*

—Lewis Carroll

S ome of us waited too long to answer that question. Shifting
our weight from one high-heeled foot to the other, we vas-
cillated. We looked so pretty in our disco dresses. Wouldn't
there always be some man wanting to dance with us?

Now the question is no longer being asked—no longer being
asked of us.

Do you remember the go-go girls who danced in cages? They
wore white vinyl boots and miniskirts or danced bikini-clad and
barefoot. I recall sitting in a club with my then husband and his
brother and watching a young woman in a tiny white bikini dance
barefoot in a cage with red velvet bars. Her hair was long and
blond; her lips and toenails were bright pink; and she looked mildly
surprised, as if she had never meant to end up in a cage suspended
over our heads. But she danced gamely on to the recorded beat of
"Windy." She had, after all, agreed to dance alone in a cage.

Most of the single women I know remind me of her now.

Maybe they planned to marry or remarry eventually. Eventually
came and they were still alone, mildly surprised, but honoring the
terms of a contract they had surely understood as well as the go-
go girl had understood the terms of her employment. What was
once a choice is now a fact of life. They are beginning to perceive
the steel under the velvet bars of the cage, the bars that say, "This
is where you live because no man has chosen you—not because you

have chosen no one." And they keep on dancing because dancing is what they do.

Maybe they didn't mean to marry or remarry—and don't want to marry now—but like my forty-year-old friend Jillian they wish they still had a *choice*. "I wish some man out there might be at least momentarily disappointed to hear I'm not looking for a husband," she says.

After the sexual revolution of the 1960s, after the decade of women of the 1970s, why have we apparently been left with such limited options? How did that happen to a generation who grew up believing the one thing we had, would always have, as one of our inalienable rights was—*choice?*

I was one of those women who broke free of a constraining marriage in the seventies. It was 1976, that symbolic year, the year I also turned thirty. There were fireworks going off in my head. My husband and I were divorced in late June, but we spent the Fourth of July together. He still couldn't understand what was happening to us; and he couldn't imagine facing a holiday without a wife. I drank too much wine and danced on the brick patio with other men. The Eagles—"Life in the Fast Lane"—were playing on the stereo. That was before the sexual revolution had let us all down, before feminism became postfeminism, when I still behaved like a girl who thought she could grow up to be president.

I told people I got divorced because I didn't like being second and being a wife meant being second. At least it did for me at that time and in that marriage. I am part of the generation who personalized politics and politicized our personal lives. The assassinations of Bobby Kennedy and Martin Luther King, Jr., the Vietnam War, and the women's movement had as much to do with my divorce as sex or money or household chores. My husband believed things I didn't: Women were different, special, separate. *Second.*

Not too long ago I gave a forty-one-year-old man of whom I'm very fond this explanation; and he said, "But, Susan, it has ever been thus. Women *are* second." His eyes were serenely incredulous; and I looked into them across a gender gap we can't pin on Ronald Reagan. On July 4, 1976, I didn't anticipate the same gap eight years later with yet another man. The choices were all mine; I chose equality.

I also chose to share custody of our only son, Richard, then eight, with his father, also Richard. Because these were idealistic times, I said, "Children are not chattel owned by their mothers." I thought his father had as much right to be a continuing part of Richard's life as I did. I was wrong about a lot of the things I believed and assumed in those days, but I was not wrong about that. Shared custody was the most right life decision I've ever made; and ironically it has given Richard and me an equality in divorce we never had in marriage. We respect each other now.

Joint custody has also given me more freedom—and left me with more remaining choices—than most divorced mothers have.

Many of the women I know who divorced in the 1970s married again because they felt marriage was the only choice. Some of them married because they didn't earn enough money—or collect enough child support—to care for their children. Some of them married because they really thought they'd found in the second husband everything they were missing in the first. But even for them the lure of the second was, in part, fatter income. They had been alone and poor; and they'd hated it, especially for their children.

Yet many are divorced again or profess to being unhappily married for the second time.

One remarried friend recently told me over a happy-hour glass of white wine, "Don't ever get married again. *You* don't have to." She meant my child was not denied through divorce his Nike shoes and designer jeans—as hers had been. While she talked, she was shredding a cocktail napkin; and for the first time I noticed the wrinkles around her eyes. When I got home and took a good look at my eyes, I had the same wrinkles in exactly the same places. What I didn't have was her emerald ring and the Cartier tank watch. She lives in a high-rent cage and envies me my life.

She said, "I heard that old Bread song about freedom on the radio the other day, and I thought about you. You're the only one who managed to get free."

I'm not so sure. "Free" implies a choice—to be single *or* married—a choice I don't really think, at thirty-eight, I have anymore.

According to the 1982 Census Bureau figures, 36 percent—or 60 million—Americans between the ages of twenty and fifty-nine are single. Of those 60 million, 26 million are men, 34 million are women. We outnumber men by 8 million.

Although there is (according to a recent Princeton study) a greater ratio of men to women in the twenty-to-twenty-four age group, the odds, from a woman's standpoint, worsen as we age. There are only 62 men for every 100 women between the ages of thirty and thirty-four, only 43 per 100 between the ages of forty and forty-four. In Boston, there are 33,500 more single women than men. In Manhattan, the ratio of single women to single men is now estimated at seven to one, not including homosexuals, which reduces the odds still further. And, the older men are, the more they prefer younger women. Can you imagine the odds against a forty-year-old woman living in Manhattan and finding love? Well, they aren't a lot better in small towns, like my hometown, Edwardsville, Illinois, population 11,000—where everyone seems to be married except a bunch of women over thirty.

I know single women who desperately want a husband and can't find a suitable mate, who desperately want a date and can't even find that. The advice books tell them, Don't be so picky. Find someone younger, shorter, less educated, poorer. Some of the advice is good, but some of it sounds dangerously like, Settle for whatever you can get. *Settle*. How foreign that word sounds to women who came of age during an era of seemingly unprecedented personal choice.

Yet I really don't believe single women are less happy than our married sisters.

Unhappiness just takes a different form when you live alone. Instead of focusing on what is there—the things about a man you cannot bear for another minute—you focus on what is missing: companionship, affection, sex, money. You tell yourself a man could solve all your problems, whereas married women secretly believe a man is the cause of all their problems. My married friend who was shredding her cocktail napkin kept saying, "If I just hadn't married.... If I just hadn't married *him*...."

Jillian doesn't agree with me. She says, "Single women are less happy because they have less money and less choice."

Even the image of the single woman isn't what it used to be, she says.

In the 1970s, the single woman was glamorous and brave. Jill Clayburgh, the single woman's cinematic patron saint, walked away from men in her movies. She always found herself. And we knew another man would be waiting when she stretched out her hand to touch him. In real life we are discovering that there is no man waiting when we finally reach out. Four out of five divorced men remarry; only three out of five women do. The odds of a woman remarrying decline as her age increases, but that is not the case for a man.

No wonder they aren't making movies about us anymore. We have become the stuff of television documentaries—serious stories about "the nouveau poor class," women and dependent children—not glamorous films. Some of us can't meet the minimum balance on our MasterCards. Some of us can't get MasterCards. And some of us can't even get laid.

We are, Jillian says, like the extra girls at the sock hop, dancing with each other because there aren't enough boys to go around. "Nobody ever looked at those girls; and nobody really looks at us now." After a certain age, women become invisible unless they are living with, dancing with, men. We are reaching that age.

Jillian complains, but she would turn down the next offer of marriage. And I would make the same choice today I made in 1976. The worst kind of loneliness is the kind you share with someone else, someone who isn't supposed to make you feel that way. Emerald rings are no more capable of dispelling that loneliness than magic ruby slippers can get you back to Kansas. When I left my marriage, I never wanted to feel that loneliness again; and I haven't. In those first few months alone, I carried an image in my head: an image of the woman I wanted to be. She was cool and professionally competent. Her answering machine recorded business messages. She had affairs with men like Mr. Spock and Robert Redford. No man touched her at the core. She was Mary Tyler Moore—only more so.

Well, I am the woman I wanted to be, but she is not without ambivalence. Sometimes I wish a man could touch me. Sometimes I wish I were the kind of woman who can look into the eyes of that forty-one-year-old chauvinist and love him anyway, but I'm not. I no longer believe—as I did in the 1970s—in a possible He, in the zipless fuck, or great sex with a stranger, or in Jill Clayburgh. She got married and had a baby.

The women in this book are still living without men. Jillian sees them—us—as a great amorphous mass, the unchosen girls at a sock hop. Most of us are the baby boomers, the generation that did everything en masse. And we certainly didn't listen to our mothers when they told us to get a husband or keep one while we could. We tried to find our own answers, different than our mothers' answers, through cultural group think.

In the 1960s we sought salvation through sex and political commitment. In the 1970s we discovered that sexual freedom had only meant we were free to be sex kittens: go-go girls, Jane Fonda playing Barbarella. In the antiwar movement, we had followed men; and when the movement was over, a lot of those men collapsed inside themselves. We went into the 1980s pinning our hopes on careers, not men, not sex, not causes other than our own. The women's network movement, the big push of the late seventies, early eighties, was about using each other to get what we wanted, about measuring very carefully what we could get in exchange for what we had to give. It was about bottom-line profit—not idealism. We thought we had grown up.

We set new standards for women. We established a new role model: She wore a Superwoman cape over her business suit and she "had it all." Ironically, the mythology we created around the new woman has given us all more work to do and has made it possible for older men to leave their wives without guilt—or adequate financial compensation.

We also created a new single class; and like everything else we have made, it does not entirely please us.

Now we are left alone, an isolated condition that some of us find rewarding, some satisfactory, some empty, but nearly all find strange. For the first time we are not on the cutting edge of our times. The 1980s celebrate marriage and late motherhood and the return of romance and traditional values—and we are left out of the celebration, alone, apart, outside.

Jillian sees us as a mass of women, which indicates a unity of experience, a solidarity of purpose, a sisterhood that may not still exist.

I see us, one by one, women in single cages, dancing alone, looking surprised.

2

The Single Woman:
A Historical Perspective

The real trouble about women is that they must always go on trying to adapt themselves to men's theories of women.

—D. H. Lawrence

In the nineteenth century, single women *were* a solid group.

A bright, independent woman sometimes chose not to marry. She turned down proposals because she had seen her sisters die in childbirth—or age prematurely under the weight of frequent pregnancies and household toil. Or she may have refused her beaux because she chose to devote her life to a career or a cause, socially acceptable alternatives to marriage.

Lee Virginia Chambers-Schiller, an assistant professor of history at the University of Colorado, has written a book about our early sisters: *Liberty, a Better Husband: Single Women in America: The Generations of 1780–1840* (Yale University Press).

While researching her subject, Chambers-Schiller was surprised to learn how much these women were admired by their families and society. They were teachers, doctors, writers, lecturers. It was even common for single women to adopt orphaned children and raise them as their own. Spinsters helped organize and lead the opposition against slavery. In fact, most of the fund raising, writing, and speaking against slavery was done by unmarried women.

The state of female celibacy was glorified just as priestly celibacy is now. Being single meant being independent—but it also meant being consecrated to a higher cause than fulfilling sexual needs. Female celibacy was seen in a positive spiritual light.

Obviously, some of those women lived together or formed strong lasting relationships with each other. The letters they exchanged were passionate, loving—and raise the question of lesbianism in the minds of twentieth-century readers. Do their letters show evidence of sexual love—or do they merely express in writing the emotional excesses of a period?

Lesbianism wasn't discussed openly then, so we can only wonder if those early spinsters found release from their celibacy in each other's arms or not. They had little opportunity for affairs with men, even discreet ones, without losing public respect or risking pregnancy. But no one wondered aloud then. No stigma was attached to being single in those pre-Freudian days. Women weren't supposed to like sex anyway—only to suffer it for the sake of their husband and procreation.

Then gradually attitudes toward unmarried women began to change. By the 1880s, a "Boston marriage" was a common term for two women who lived together. Its meaning was suspect. A close reading of Henry James's *The Bostonians* shows definite lesbian undertones in the relationship between Olive Chancellor, the middle-aged feminist fighting a southern gentleman (Basil Ransom) for the soul of young Verena Tarrant. Feminism and lesbianism were becoming associated in the public mind.

Chambers-Schiller theorizes that spinsterhood began getting a bad name at the turn of the century because "men began to get frightened at how happy and successful these single women were. They felt threatened."

By the early 1900s, "spinsters" had become women who couldn't "catch" a husband. They were the old-maid aunts who had to live in the homes of sisters and brothers, where they were only tolerated. They were "eccentric" at best—and downright crazy at worst.

The single woman's image didn't improve again until the depression and the Second World War.

In the twentieth century, whenever there was a good reason for women to work—helping indigent or ill parents, supporting the war effort, supporting a family after the death of a husband—or there was a shortage of marriageable men, being single was acceptable.

Often those working single women married their jobs instead of men.

Marie, seventy-three, a retired accountant–office manager for a construction firm in Belleville, Illinois, was one of those women. She worked for that same firm for forty-seven years, from age eighteen to sixty-five. When she retired, she was given company stock and a seat on the board in recognition of her loyalty and service. This family-owned company is her "family" too.

She says, "In 1929, you were lucky to get a job. I was eighteen then and just out of high school. I was glad to be hired. I did everything. I was the secretary and the bookkeeper and I cleaned the floors too. My parents raised me to think your job comes first; and mine always did.

"During the depression, there were so many people out of work, if you didn't put your job first, well, others would. If it took until ten or eleven or twelve at night, you did it. I didn't have time to think about finding a man.

"I started at $12 a week. Mr. Brandon, the founder, was still here. He was such a good man. He had learned to write in German; and I was the only one who could decipher his scrawls. The Brandons have all been good to me. They are people of their word. This company has been my home and my family.

"No, I'm not sorry I didn't marry. You see these diamond rings on my fingers, this diamond watch? I bought them for myself. But I never thought of myself as a career woman like women do today. I had responsibility; and I made good money—but I always knew how things were supposed to be."

Marie has her hair done once a week. She visits the company often; and everyone treats her with affection and respect. She says, "I trained most of these girls," about women who are old enough to be grandmothers. And the president of the company calls her when he needs to know anything about the business's history.

If she were somebody's mother, grandmother—could her place in that family circle be as comfortable and secure as it is in this one?

Marie can't remember exactly when it was that she knew she wasn't going to be a wife and mother.

"There was a time in the late thirties, early forties when the company had an office in Indiana. I spent a lot of time going back and forth between the two offices. I guess I already knew by then I wouldn't get married when I was always running back and forth like that. But it didn't make a difference. I was the person the Brandons trusted to check the books, to make sure everything was okay. They needed me."

Nobody told Marie she could, and *should*, have it all. For her, the choice was simple: If you had a career, a real career, you didn't have a husband and a family. And you didn't tell yourself you could change your mind and find a husband late and at forty mother a child. It was over, the choice made, everything settled, much sooner than forty or even thirty. And you lived with the choice. Single women worked, and married women seldom did.

Those were the rules until women entered the workplace in large numbers in the 1960s. By the 1970s we had realized that men have it all—jobs and marriage, success and love, active lives and children—and we said, "We should have it too." So we set out to get it.

Many of us delayed marriage to launch careers, as men have traditionally done. Nobody pointed out that the men our age would be married to someone else, or looking for someone younger, by the time we were established professionally.

And some of us already had the marriage and the children when we were told we could go for it all. Some of the old husbands didn't fit into the new life-styles. So we got divorced.

Thus single women in the 1980s are not one unified class like those spinsters who never wed, never mothered, and never really thought they would. We are two separate groups: the never married and the formerly married. And two factors set us apart: biological optimism and money.

If we have never married, we are optimistic about the prospects for maternity into our forties. If we married young and had our children, then divorced, we believe by thirty-five we are too "old" to do it again.

If we have never married, we have more disposable income than divorced mothers struggling to provide our kids with a middle-class life-style on one, usually inadequate, salary.

3

Single Women and Sex: Where We Have Been

The zipless fuck was more than a fuck. It was a platonic ideal. Zipless because when you came together zippers fell away like rose petals, underwear blew off in one breath like dandelion fluff. . . . For the true, ultimate zip-less A-1 fuck, it was necessary that you never get to know the man very well.

—from *Fear of Flying* (1973)
by Erica Jong

By the time Jong wrote those words, we were romanticizing sex, not romance. We believed in sex, not love. What we wanted from each other was sexual freedom, not commitment.

The roots of the modern women's movement lie in the sexual revolution of the 1960s and the work-place revolution of the 1970s. But the sexual revolution *had* to come first. In the dissatisfaction of the current moment, one cannot dismiss its tremendous impact on women of the baby-boom generation: Sexual freedom eliminated one pressing reason for marriage—physical gratification. We no longer had to be married to have sex. That, coupled with the pill, allowed us for the first time in history to triumph over our own biology.

When it was no longer necessary for us to be safely wed the moment our lust became unbearable, the delicious possibilities open to us seemed limitless. The freedom to scratch our sexual itches whenever and with whomever we pleased really led to the freedom to concentrate on building our careers.

Without easy sex and easier birth control, the new single class could not have been. Once we didn't have to marry each other, men and women alike were in no hurry to find legal partners. When Jong introduced Isadora in 1973, we believed that sex in marriage was inevitably disappointing. We equated marital sex with boredom. As countless books and magazine articles had reported, husbands were notoriously deficient in meeting the sexual needs of wives. So we thought men who were not pledged to us, who did not love and care for us, would be better to us in bed.

If single, we saw no reason to marry, since we didn't yet want children. If married, we were beginning to see plenty of reasons for getting divorced. And one of those reasons was sex.

In another time, sexually dissatisfied young wives baked more cakes, trimmed more hats, had more babies—*sublimated*. Not us. Nobody had ever told us we couldn't have what we wanted; and we wanted good sex.

Kara and I, both WASPs raised in small southern Illinois towns, arrived via different routes at the same place—both psychologically and geographically. We live across the hall from each other in a four-unit apartment building in need of paint on the white trim, with rusting fake colonial columns on the porch and an unmown lawn. Privately owned, this building stands out in a neighborhood of well-tended apartment complexes all owned by the same developer—who excludes us from his swimming pool, of course. The rent is the lowest in the area. We still don't pay it on time.

The lawn really bothers Kara. So does the dirty hallway. Once this summer she borrowed a lawnmower from a friend and cut the grass herself. We tenants take turns vacuuming the stairs and mopping the hall. We are all unmarried: Paula, divorced, who lives with her eight-year-old son downstairs; Dock, almost divorced, our token male, who lives with his six-year-old son across from Paula; Kara, never married, over Dock; Richie and I live over Paula. Often we adults stand in the hallway and complain about the landlord. It's our form of small talk. When Kara isn't with us, we are just as likely to talk about why our marriages didn't work out as the unpainted walls.

Kara and I often stand in the upstairs hall, which separates our apartments, pulling dead leaves off the scraggly philodendrons in the planter and talking about men and sex.

None of us plan to stay here, but none of us has anywhere else to go either. "I know you're going to leave before I do—and then I'll hate being here without you," Kara says. I would hate being here without her too.

We are a little like sorority sisters staying in a tacky old building and plotting what we'll do when we live in the real world, how we'll spend money, what kinds of things we'll buy. We have subscriptions to catalogues full of beautiful clothing and gifts: I. Magnin, Bloomingdale's, Neiman-Marcus. Once in a while we buy something we can't afford. The difference between us and sorority sisters is they know they'll marry a rich man.

And we know we won't.

We know exactly what it is we're going to get out of men: what we've gotten in the past, sex. We insist, at least, that the sex be good.

Kara and I went to see the film *Star 80* together in the spring of 1984. She watched the story of playmate Dorothy Stratten's life and death with growing discomfort. Before the movie was quite finished—after Stratten's husband, Paul Snyder, had brutally murdered her and before he had killed himself with the same enormous gun he had just used to blow her head away—Kara stood up. "I've got to get out of here," she said.

I followed her into the ladies room. "That was awful," she said. "Disgusting." Her anger was palpable. I could feel it prickly on my skin like the beginnings of a rash.

"She should have been smart enough not to go back," I said. "She should have *known*." I thought her anger was directed as much at Stratten for her stupidity as Snyder for his crime—because mine would have been. And I was wrong.

Kara combed her fine blond hair—which she still wears long with Alice-in-Wonderland bangs and chews when she's nervous—and poured water into the yellow plastic cup she always carries in her handbag. She's a chain smoker; and she still does grass. Her mouth must always be dry. At thirty-five, she could pass for eighteen were it not for the tiny lines around her eyes. They make her look twenty-five. She weighs less than a hundred pounds. One would not expect her to talk about men in terms of their "dick size"—she is too blue-eyed, tiny-pure to talk like that, but she does. At this point in my life, she is my closest friend. I trust her. Neither one of us trusts men.

On the way home, she told me she understood why Dorothy went back, why she didn't know what was going to happen to her, or if she was dimly aware, why she accepted her fate.

"How could anyone be so purely dumb?" I asked. Stratten was, in my snap feminist analysis, dumb. A classic female victim. She was used by Snyder, who found her working in a Dairy Queen in Vancouver, British Columbia, when she was seventeen, seduced her, talked her into posing nude, then sent her photos to *Playboy*. She was victimized by the Bunny system and the Hollywood machine. But she was a willing victim, who held on to her own naivete; an appallingly sweet, wholesome woman who put her faith in the men who used her body to make a buck. She called Hugh Hefner "Mr. Hefner." She apparently went to see Snyder one last time because she thought she could make him understand why she wanted a divorce.

How could anyone be so purely dumb?

It's a question I have often asked—and usually asked about women whose lives I didn't know, a question that sums up the difference between Kara and me. She was young and single and alone in the trenches of the sexual revolution. I was married to a very nice man, taking small risks or none at all, dipping my toes in the sanitized water of heated chlorine pools.

I didn't understand how some women could stay with men who beat them and others could put themselves in positions where they might be raped. I didn't understand them any more than a devout Catholic mother married to a wealthy doctor understands the need some women have for an abortion. Kara understood it all.

"Well, it can happen pretty easy," she said. "It happened to me. I mean I wasn't in *Playboy* and I didn't get shot, but still . . ."

She told me about the time she'd impulsively hitched to meet friends in Mexico City in the late 1960s—when she was about the same age as Dorothy had been as a Dairy Queen counter girl. She arrived after the banks were closed with very little cash in her wallet. And she couldn't find her friends.

"Well, it's impossible to cash a check there until the banks open. So I knew I had to stay up all night. I thought I could handle that, if I kept going from one respectable coffee shop to another.

"A group of men trailed me from one place to the next. An American woman—a blonde, a student, dirty from the road—alone in the middle of the night in Mexico City. That's something to follow. You know what they thought I was.

"You could almost hear them licking their lips.

"So there was this one particular guy, a real creep. Very pushy. He sat down next to me at Denny's and tried to strike up a conversation. I told him to go away.

"He followed me to the next coffee shop. I more or less let him sit with me. It sounds crazy, but I felt a little safer because he was with me. This whole pack of men was hanging around outside. They were leering at me through the window. I thought if I let this one stay, the others would leave me alone.

"It was about 4:00 A.M. I was so tired; and this guy was such an awful creep. I kept getting bad vibrations from him; and the vibrations signaled violence.

"I *knew* he was someone who could, who probably had, hurt women.

"But I was so tired. I knew he could bargain for me in the cheap section of the city for a hotel room I could afford. I told him I'd pay his cab fare back if he would. He agreed.

"At this hotel I made it clear to the clerk the room was for *one;* and this guy haggled the price down like he'd promised. He walked me to the room, took the key from my hand.

"I should have run, but I went inside with him. I told him, 'You have to get out of here; and I'm not going to sleep with you.'

"He picked me up and threw me across the room. He grabbed me by the arm, pulled me up, and slammed me down on the bed. Suddenly he was on top of me; and I screamed as loud as I could. He smacked me hard across the face, but I kept screaming.

"Two men were beating on the door. Somehow they got it open and pulled this guy off me. The next day I had a swollen face and a black eye. I should have known. I should have seen it coming. Maybe I did.

"So I guess I know what happened to Dorothy Stratten. She felt shackled to this creep, knowing he was a creep, an absolutely slimy being trying to pull her down. But she still felt she owed him something, some kind of explanation. She still thought she could *talk* to him. You can see how it happened, can't you?"

Now I can see how it happened.

Now I can imagine being young and alone, blond and pretty, in a place where there is no longer a good reason or a valid excuse for saying no, where men circle you, and you accept being the prey. They see breasts unfettered by a bra beneath a tie-dyed T-shirt, an ass distractingly displayed in tight jeans threadbare under the cheeks. Do they take no for an answer? Do you want them to accept your refusal—or do you believe putting yourself on the line is the cost of this new freedom, this freedom to fuck?

Now I can see how it happened, because Kara has made me see it, but it wasn't my experience at all.

While Kara was in Mexico, I was changing diapers. My six-month-old baby was spitting up on my Mother's Day gardenia corsage while I held him on my lap during mass. My husband's parents were calling *my* baby "Richard's baby." I was learning I could earn familial approval on both sides by "being a good mother," if I didn't leave my baby with a sitter too often or allow him to linger in soiled clothes in his playpen. Chafing and crying all the while, I was learning a lot about being second.

And so was Kara, though her lesson was more brutal.

We were, in the vernacular of our times, coming from different places. I was a suburban mother who thought boredom was the worst thing that could happen to me; and it was happening. Kara was in Mexico being attacked.

We stood in the hallway and talked for a long time the night we saw *Star 80*. Kara was angry; and anger energizes her.

Soon we were bitching—as we frequently are—about men. We begin with the specific, one man and one complaint about him, and then generalize: *men*. Men are so damned———— (fill in the blank).

If I ever fall in love I won't be as close to Kara as I am now. Loving a man would come between us. Neither one of us has loved a man in the all-consuming way most women say they have loved. We love the way men do: giving part, but not all, of ourselves, of our time and devotion and care. We are a little proud of that.

She is fairly contemptuous of those women who give so much. When a woman friend marries, she moves into a realm Kara doesn't understand. They aren't so close anymore.

She wouldn't care if I went to bed with one of her lovers; we could handle that. We could depersonalize him to the point where he was merely a vibrator we had shared. She would probably ask me how it felt. Men are for sex. For a limited amount of companionship. She likes having them around, but not too frequently. Men are for show too: They are escorts to take to dinner at her brother's, her brother who thinks she should marry.

Men already have too much power, so she is careful not to give them any more.

"When I was very little, I remember seeing my father's penis, flashing by," Kara says. "He was naked, probably dashing from the shower; and I saw him. I was careful not to stare. It was just something out of the corner of my eye. I didn't want him to know I'd seen it. I didn't want him to have something else over me, something else he had that I didn't.''

Her parents divorced when Kara was twelve and her brother, Bob, thirteen. They were told to choose a parent. Bob chose to live with their father; she chose their mother.

"My dad never forgave me. The funny thing is Bob doesn't remember we had to choose. He thinks they did it for us, they decided where we'd go. Anyway Mom forgave him."

Her mother lived with a man for sixteen years before she married him. And then she did it because her grandchildren were getting old enough to "ask questions." When they married last summer, Kara and I picked out her wedding dress and mailed it to her. She said it was "fine."

"I guess she was scared," Kara says. "But really it's like she was married for those sixteen years. She never went out with anyone else. She acted like a wife."

Kara says she learned in childhood "marriage isn't such a good idea. I saw it didn't work, and I didn't want anything to do with it."

She also learned how to get along with men.

"I stayed a virgin through high school even though I was horny. I saw it was the way to have long relationships with boys. I watched what they did to other girls. As soon as they had sex with a girl, it was over. And they talked to all their friends, bragged about who they'd had. So I wouldn't put out, not until I got out of high school, not until I got out of that."

She has been raped. More than once. But she says, "They really can't touch you. I learned that. It's only your body. If they don't hurt you physically, they can't really get you. I was scared to death of being cut. When that didn't happen, I knew I had not really been touched. It was only sex."

In Mexico a man who was sleeping with her friend climbed in

bed with her one night. When she said No, he "did it anyway." She lay still, pretending to be asleep. What irritated her most was his attitude the next day. "He seemed to think we had done it *together*."

The women who did not make safe early marriages were more exposed to the brutality of sex than the rest of us. Yes, any woman can be raped. Even by a "friend." But rape is most likely to happen to the more vulnerable, the less protected—to women alone.

It leaves a legacy: anger, bitterness, distrust, social concern.

Kara is a volunteer on the rape crisis hotline. Sometimes when I knock on her door, she answers with the phone in hand. She isn't speaking. Someone on the other end is. Her face is pale. I'm sure this must be a hotline call, but she doesn't talk about it very often. Sometimes, much later, long after the call, she will say, "I had this call from a young girl. It was her father." Or stepfather. Mother's boyfriend. Uncle.

"Sometimes you wonder, if it was bad . . . if she'll ever be able to enjoy sex."

Because I didn't know Kara when she was very young, I really don't know if she ever romanticized men and sex.

Her first love, she recalls, "had a disappointingly small cock. I remember seeing it and thinking, That's it? And later when he insisted we'd done it, I wanted to ask him, 'That was it? That's what it's all about? That little bit of pressure against my cunt?'

"I didn't ask him, but I looked so shocked, I guess, that he said no, we hadn't done it after all. We'd just come close. I think he was embarrassed. I think that was actually it; and I lost my virginity without even feeling it."

Neither one of us had traumatic deflowering stories. I remember clearly when my hymen broke: I was twelve years old and climbing a tree (the same tree that would give me my first orgasm at thirteen while I was shimmying down it). I felt something tear inside and later found a piece of tough skin hanging out my vagina. My sister, Ginny, explained what had happened.

"Technically," she said, "you're not a virgin anymore."

We both laughed. Deflowered by a tree.

As Kara did, I remained a (nontechnical) virgin in high school too. Obviously, I did not fear penetration. Nor by senior year did I care about my "reputation." I was ready, but my steady, David, thought we should wait.

I was eighteen and Roger, my first love, was eighteen when we finally did "it." He had read books; and so he diligently applied himself to "foreplay," which was largely finger-fucking, to "expand the opening." Roger was not a disappointment. Kara envied me the experience until I told her he died the following year. He killed himself.

There were men, "boys, really," who wanted to marry Kara when she was eighteen, nineteen, twenty. She was never so "overpowered by one of them in bed" that she thought it was worthwhile. In those years, she was doing drugs; and drugs were usually better than sex. She was a risk taker.

"I was willing to try anything, even if I was afraid. The first time I dropped acid, I was scared to death, but I'd do anything once, especially if it scared me."

I was never so brave. When I met Richard and he was handsome and the sex led to orgasm for both of us, I married him. Marriage was the way out from under my mother's voluminous protective wings. And I didn't know enough about sex, or the pleasure capacity of my own body, to know that just having orgasms, one at a time, wasn't really good enough.

"It takes a while for me to get off," Kara says. "And I really need a good cock to finish."

It takes me not long at all to "get off"—which may be the reason I married young and she didn't. I confused the orgasmic rush with love. The books about multiple orgasms weren't published in time to save me.

Yet she didn't plan *not* to be married, not at that point in her life.

"I thought I would be married someday, it would probably happen. I was in no hurry for it to happen. But I never thought I would always be single, because everyone eventually got married, didn't they? Isn't that what we grew up thinking?

"It was just beginning to be fashionable to put off getting married, to keep your options open—and that was fine with me."

Paradoxically, though I said the same "till death do us part" vow every other married person said, I didn't believe my options were closed either. The clearest memory of my wedding day is what was going on in my head as I walked down the aisle in my white satin dress with the floor-length lace mantilla billowing around me: "No.

No way is this going to be forever, for the rest of my life. *No.*"

I said "I do" because that's what young women wearing white dresses have traditionally said in front of altars in churches. But in my mind, at least, the choices were still there.

Kara and I both chose one path without ever thinking we could not someday choose the other.

"The sex was never good for long," she says about her early lovers.

The sex wasn't good for long in my marriage either—even though I was reading *Redbook* and doing all I could to turn on my man. I masturbated a lot (which *Redbook* did not tell me to do, but *Ms.* said was all right); and of course I never told my good Catholic husband, who believed masturbation was wrong, that I did.

My first significant extramarital affair (at twenty-six) was conducted largely long-distance via the mails. Though I had that charter subscription to the fledgling *Ms.*, I was still romanticizing sex long after Kara must have been *very* worldly-wise about it. I met a twenty-one-year-old Wisconsin poet who was visiting St. Louis. When he went back home, he wrote passionate letters, each containing a poem. And I was very bored.

Whenever we got together, his body failed to deliver on the promises he had written. I suspect he was a homosexual who hadn't yet come out of the closet. At that time, I just thought he was too incredibly sensitive to feel comfortable making love to a married woman.

I spent the New Year's holiday of 1972–73 in Wisconsin with him. Richard and my best friend, Barb, drove me to the airport. Of course Richard paid for the ticket. That was, Barb said later, the weirdest experience of her life. While we were waiting for the plane, which was late, the three of us plus five-year-old Richie and her three-year-old son, Mikie, wandered through airport boutiques. Richard asked me if I would stay home in exchange for anything, everything, I wanted in the boutiques.

No. I chose to spend the weekend with a kid who slept on a mattress on the floor. Spider plants hung in the curtainless windows where the setting sun poured relentlessly in every afternoon. We rolled around on the mattress a lot, but he never had an orgasm.

His best friend, a tall, handsome and very macho journalist, spent New Year's Eve with us. After the poet had too much to drink and passed out, his friend and I stayed up all night and talked. He was far too loyal a friend to take advantage of the situation, but he did play with my breasts—giving me the most genuinely erotic moments I ever experienced in Wisconsin.

Back home in Illinois, I read Erica Jong's first novel, *Fear of Flying*. I made all my friends read it. "We are entitled to good sex," I told them.

And Jong told us we didn't have to "fall in love" to get it. She gave us the perfect fantasy: the zipless fuck, the intensely gratifying sexual encounter with a stranger. It was a fantasy I was more than ready to adopt. Sex without commitment—without guilt.

Richard said I would be sorry someday if I lived in a world where men no longer opened doors for me. It was something a lot of husbands were saying at the time. But the women's movement had made me realize I was missing the sexual revolution, had given me this sense of sexual entitlement. I *deserved* multiple orgasms and oral sex.

Kara and I agree that few men are good at performing oral sex. They're fond of having it done, but not of doing it. Actually, I feel the same way.

She says, "I get turned on doing it too. But I really begin to resent it when I've been with a guy for a while, and he won't go down on me."

We have known few men who enthusiastically go down. When I found one who did, my marriage was over.

He was twenty years my senior, in nice though not spectacular shape, and extremely skilled in bed. We rendezvoused at the Howard Johnson's Motel off the Hampton Avenue exit at I-44 in St. Louis. He was a professor; and he couldn't afford more pleasing accommodations. I had my first oral orgasm atop one of those hideous orange chenille spreads; it was early March, almost my thirtieth birthday. And suddenly I had to be free—though certainly not to marry him.

I was delighted with what he taught me about my body—and then I was angry at all the men who'd used it before him, without giving me so much in return.

How many other women must have had similar experiences?

No wonder there was so much anger directed against men in the early days of the movement. One by one, we were discovering that we had been had, on the home front, in the workplace, in bed. Powerful women writers, Kate Millet, Germaine Greer, Gloria Steinem, and others, were painfully detailing for us exactly *how* we had been had. At that point, we were only blaming men, not ourselves.

One of their messages was: We are responsible for our own orgasms now. We don't need permission from men to have them.

And the problem with so many of our marriages was that our husbands still thought we *did* need their permission.

It was a good time to be single. Men were the enemy. Men were to be used for pleasure, just as they had used us.

Kara and I got to the sexual revolution via different paths. She met strange men in foreign lands, while I went to bed with other women's husbands whom I met through the Catholic Parents Club. Mine was certainly a less arduous, less direct route. Marriage preserves innocence; and I was innocent until I was no longer married.

When I was no longer married, I found it easy to share Kara's philosophy: Don't trust men; only sleep with them.

The experience of multiple partners led us both to the same obvious conclusion: There would always be someone new, someone better, some other man to make love to us, so why not leave when a relationship grew boring or difficult or too complicated? It was what men deserved anyway.

Why limit ourselves to one man when lots of men were available?

I got divorced so that I could join the generation of women, my generation, who kept their options open, put their own needs first, and considered sex a natural right. Together with the men of our generation, we weren't very good at "working things out," but we were certainly wonderful at "moving on." We knew how to break up. Our music about breaking up and moving on was upbeat and positive. The civilized divorce was surely our invention.

Settle was not a word we used. When Jim Morrison and the Doors sang "Light My Fire," we sang with them. "Set the night on fire" or get out of my bed was our group's sexual motto.

We also talked a lot.

I said that good talk and good sex were the things I wanted from a man, not financial support, not identity, not presents and lavish meals or trips. Just talk and sex. Sex and talk.

We had plenty of both in the 1970s. I talked my way out of several relationships. So did Kara.

She never saw any reason to give a man—a penis—power over her by marrying him. Somewhere along the way, she even stopped thinking about marriage as a future alternative. She didn't dismiss it entirely, but she kept pushing it farther and farther away, until it was so far out of sight, she couldn't imagine being married.

"When men began talking about commitment, I got out. Making a commitment meant marriage; and for women, marriage means giving a man too much power in your life. I just knew I wasn't going to do it; and I was glad we lived in a time where a woman could have sex, all the sex she wanted, without getting married.

"I thought in vague terms of having a kid someday, of being a single mother. I didn't give up on having kids then, just marriage."

We chose sex, not marriage.

Did anyone say we couldn't change our minds—again?

4

Single Women and Sex: Where We Are Now

Sex with love is the greatest thing in life—but sex without love, that's not so bad either.

—Mae West

What would Mae West make of the mid-1980s? To date, the 1980s have been a humorless, sexless period, largely defined by yuppies and the New Right, two serious groups of people who have more in common than allegiance to Ronald Reagan. They also don't believe in sex without love.

Ms. magazine, Jerry Falwell, and the Vatican are all opposed to casual sex and pornography.

In their February 1984 issue, *Ms.* told us, "The 'zipless fuck' sounded like a great idea at the time, but whether out of biologically or culturally conditioned differences, casual sex has simply not worked out for most of us." "Us" meaning women.

Why not? Because we need "trust" and "commitment." Because we still "intertwine" the "romantic and the erotic." Because we get pregnant and men don't—which *Ladies Home Journal* knew a hundred years ago. The sexual revolution was a bust because we "lost our right to say, 'No.'" *Lost* it? Didn't we give it away—eagerly handing it to men as we have handed them so many other gifts?

In 1974, when *Fear of Flying* came out in paperback, who would have predicted that a decade later feminists would be discovering that women get pregnant and men don't, that we have a right to say no? In those first adventures of Isadora Wing, pregnancy was not a concern. Outrageous Isadora, the lustiest woman in modern literature, the verbal equivalent of Mae West on screen—Isadora wanted orgasms not babies.

The third Isadora book, *Parachutes and Kisses,* published in the fall of 1984, chronicles her adventures in the 1980s, when she is having far less fun in just as many beds. Her joyless affairs are conducted mostly as revenge against the man, the husband, who left her. What's happened to Isadora in ten years isn't much different than what's happened to other women: divorce, marriage, divorce.

The wrinkles have popped out around her eyes; and she is tired, disillusioned with casual sex, uneasy about being alone, afraid of growing old. Now she views her public stance of independence as a charade. Well, she was *always* desperately searching for *the* man, but somehow she fooled us and herself ten years ago: We all thought she was having more fun looking for him inside every strange pair of trousers than she actually was.

Now she tells us, "Going to bed with new men was never quite what it was touted to be."

Isadora is nothing but a reflection of her times. Sex died between 1974 and 1984. Could Isadora, forty and three times divorced, bring it back to life?

An August 1982 *Time* magazine cover story, "The New Scarlet Letter," speculated that herpes was killing the sexual revolution: "Now suddenly the old fears and doubts [about sex] are edging back. So is the fire and brimstone rhetoric of the Age of Guilt. The reason for all this dolor: Herpes."

The venereal disease, a recurring viral infection with no cure, was credited with virtually putting an end to the one-night stand. And certainly everyone talked "fear of herpes," magnifying the disease out of proportion and identifying its victims, those unlucky enough to get caught in the sexual revolution's crossfire, as social outcasts, wearers of the 1980's version of the scarlet letter. Suddenly we were all looking for health-certificate relationships.

But casual sex would have fallen into disfavor, herpes or no.

If casual sex wasn't working out for us, it wasn't really working out for men either. *Ms.* is claiming a female victory for the return to romance, a return they were deriding a few years earlier: "Could the new conservatism [of sexual attitudes] represent, at least on the surface, a way for women to gain some measure of control in their lives, to see love on our terms. . . . The new emphasis on romance may also be an attempt to put love back on an equal footing." This new woman sounds like a ward politician who backed the wrong mayoral candidate and is now scrambling to rewrite the speeches that are history.

We were not equals in the sexual revolution—but we are not equals in romance either. Women who have played the aggressor, made the phone calls, and bought the theater tickets can tell you where it usually got them. "Nowhere," Jillian says. "Men don't like to be pursued openly."

The men's magazines were the first to tell us that sex was dead. In January 1982, *Playboy* said the best sex "is in relationships." In December 1982, *Esquire* said "high monogamy," the religion of the new marriage, had replaced casual sex. In this and many other pieces done in the early 1980s *Esquire* sounded like *Seventeen* with a mustache.

New "sensitive men," those aging baby boomers now concerned about maintaining their erections, may have discovered that sexual freedom gave women, we baby boomers moving into our most sexually vigorous years, too much power. They wanted "relationships" again. Men, who had become a scarce and thus precious commodity anyway, were discovering the joys of marriage and fatherhood and one devoted woman. And women, who were determined not to be left sitting on the sidelines without partners, donned ruffles and prepared to dance to the new music.

The interesting thing about this major change in values is how it was effected. Women seem not to have noticed the 1980s have been choreographed largely by men. Maybe this is because feminists, who are prone to being uptight, have been for the most part uneasy about sex.

Has feminism ever helped us out in bed? Or has feminism only been concerned with the dangers of sex—rape and sexual harassment, unwanted pregnancy and abortion, sexual abuse and exploitation?

Now, when we greatly outnumber the available men, when we are at or near the peak of our sexual powers—we are told to *commit*. Is commitment supposed to protect us from the dangers? Can such a reactionary retreat really keep us safe?

What we need is practical advice on how to conduct guiltless affairs with younger men, older men, single men, married men; on how to handle ourselves as equals in these affairs; on how to enter them risking no more than men do and leave them losing no more than men do either. Our magazines should be telling us how to love men less and ourselves more. Instead they are telling us to fall in love and marry when quite obviously many of us will not be able to follow that advice: There simply are not enough men to go around.

Just as those happy housewives of the 1950s did, we are trying to obey the directives of our culture handed down to us in our magazines, movies, and music.

Two days before Thanksgiving I had lunch with Lynne, thirty-three, owner of a successful one-woman ad agency. We met at Kennedy's, a restaurant-bar in a renovated warehouse building on Laclede's Landing, the riverfront area in St. Louis. Never married, Jewish, very chic and attractive, Lynne has done everything: marijuana, cocaine, abortions (two), casual sex—everything except marriage and motherhood, which she is anxious to try now. I asked her how she feels about casual sex.

"I feel very bad about it now. In fact, I don't do it. Hardly ever. I do it once in a while—well, I'm talking about the last few years—like maybe out of revenge against the person I really care about or out of some overwhelming physical attraction when there's somebody I want a taste of."

"Is it good?"

"Yeah, once in a while, but it's nothing that I really want to do. If I never did it again the rest of my life, I wouldn't miss it, as long as I had somebody that I cared about. That makes a difference, if you have someone around or not. If you don't, then it is easier to talk yourself into being self-destructive."

"You think of casual sex as being destructive?"

"I really do. Because nine times out of ten I would just feel so crummy. I'd have no self-respect. When it's over, it's gone. It's not something you retain. It's done. And then you have to do it over again. So sex becomes nothing and meaningless. Yes, self-destructive, especially if it was motivated by anger.

"I never really liked doing it, but I did it plenty. And sometimes, I have to admit, it was a very enjoyable experience. I didn't always feel like I was destroying myself.

"But lately it's so dumb."

"Is it 'dumb' because you're looking for commitment now?"

"Well, yeah. I want sex to mean something, to be an expression. I like affection more now. I notice the little things. You know, if he puts his hand on my head, pats my head, that's really nice, caring. Do you know what I mean?"

"Did herpes help influence you?"

"I never gave it a thought. I never was dealing with low-life-type people."

"You think only low-life people get herpes?"

"No, you're absolutely right. That's not true. I was totally naive not to think about it, but I never really did. By the time herpes hit the papers, I was really slowing down. I had a more or less steady relationship for three years. Plain old sex alone is just not that big a deal."

"Do your friends feel the same way?"

"I still have friends who are picking up men here or there, but they're in the minority and more and more they're less and less happy about doing it. My friend Meg still does it, but she's in therapy now and coming to her senses. She's learning you don't need that if you're happy inside, you don't need to affirm your sexual desirability that way. Casual sex is just a game you play with yourself to prove someone wants you."

Only a little more than a year ago I ran into Lynne at Culpepper's, a trendy bar in the city's Central West End (an eclectic cultural blend of liberal yuppies and conservative gays). She had a pink tint to her black hair. She was dressed in pseudopunk; and she was obviously looking to get laid. When she called me the next day to say that she *had,* she said, "I like to know I can get sex when I need it."

The sex that night had been "casual," with an acquaintance, a man who had dated some of her friends, but she insisted it was "satisfactory." And revenge could not have been a motive. Her relationship with Mike had ended some months before. Mike is an alcoholic, the man who impregnated her twice and failed both times to hold her hand either during or after the abortion. On a few occasions, including one in a public place, he knocked her around. He lied to her, cheated on her, and refused to tell her he loved her until some months after they stopped seeing each other. If she wasn't over him that night at Culpepper's, she was at least aware he was gone. She had no one on whom to seek revenge.

I had known Lynne a long time and watched her go through many men and many phases; and the phases are linked inextricably to the men. She admittedly "knocks [herself] out" to please them, to become the woman each wants her to be. She has been as free, sexually and otherwise, as they expect her to be. With Mike, and more recently with John, she drank too much, did too many drugs. John, who is also in the media, took her to parties. She met Roger, the new man in her life, at one of the parties.

"Mike always took me to parties where I didn't know anyone, then left me alone. I was on my own; I had to introduce myself to people. It was like I hadn't come with anyone. The night I met Roger [three months ago], he asked Mike if we were together. Well, Mike made it quite clear we were not, not really. He hated feeling pinned down. So Roger asked me out."

She hasn't dated anyone else since. A few weeks after the first date, when she had already decided she would marry him if and when he asked, she said (over another lunch table), "I don't know about the sex. After the first time in bed with him, I thought, 'Well, I could always have affairs.'"

But over lunch at Kennedy's, she said, "I've come to terms with myself now. And when you do that, come to terms, you can have really great sex with someone. All the pieces come together. Sex isn't isolated from the rest of life, you know. All the pieces have to fit together; and sex is just a piece.

"It all goes back to how you feel about yourself. If you overeat or sleep around or drink too much or stay in a job you hate, it all comes from the same source, from inside. You don't like yourself."

Roger is forty-six, a divorced Catholic father of four children, ages eight through twelve. A lawyer and small-time politico, he has introduced her to a level of society she hasn't known, to exclusive suburban clubs—"where Jews don't belong, which makes it that much more attractive to me to get in there." She bought a new wardrobe, including a formal gown and a mink jacket, to go out with him. Now she dresses like a Jewish yuppie, but she says she'd give up her career for marriage, a marriage in which she could have a daughter, buy and sell 1950s collectibles, and redecorate Roger's home in an upper-class suburb.

A few weeks ago she called and asked me, "What does one wear to a squash demonstration?" She's taking tennis lessons. On Fridays she bakes chocolate cakes to take to his children.

Her expectations about sex have changed, she says.

"They've come down to reality. Sex is not always great. Things interfere. Sometimes affection or a nice word or a pat is all I need. I don't have to have intercourse every single time. On the other hand, if you care about someone it can be dynamite. But not every time.

"I don't take it personally anymore if he's not interested. We have an adult relationship. This is the best sexual relationship I've ever had. It's real. It's pleasant."

She insists sex is "still a priority. But love, love's important too."

"Would you do all this, make all these changes, fit yourself into someone's life the way you're doing, if the sex wasn't good?"

"I don't know. I hope not."

He's helping her, she says, to be less inhibited. "I was shy at first with men unless it was a one-night stand and I knew I'd never see the guy again. Then I could really be bold. It didn't matter. Roger's helping me overcome some inhibitions. I'm learning to like oral sex, to like performing it. That turns me on now."

"Is he that good in bed?"

"Well, he's good for me."

We women are and always have been wonderful at rationalization. We read into men's words and behaviors what we want, desperately need, to find there. Many of us are voluntarily participating in the sex backlash, the new return to romance, a state of being in which men's words and behaviors are more important to us, more closely scrutinized than before. It is part of the women's backlash, the reactionary period we should have known would follow great social upheaval. The shock is that women, rationalizing wildly, are such an eager part of the backlash against themselves.

As we flirt and bake cakes again out of fear, out of social pressure, we don't dare admit we might be taking a step backward in relinquishing some of the sexual freedom we gained in the 1960s—relinquishing some of that sexual power to men who may have been frightened by our new sexual assertiveness. Because they are in short supply, because they are as desirable as a pair of Levis in the Soviet Union—must we let them dictate the terms again?

The editors of women's magazines either believe, or pretend to believe, the return to monogamy is our idea; and maybe it was. Never married women are eager for babies now. Formerly married women are looking for someone to pay half the bills again. But the seminal book that reported this return, *The End of Sex* (1983) was written by a man, George Leonard. Yes, the same George Leonard who wrote articles, including a special issue of *Look* magazine, in the 1960s touting the sexual revolution. Apparently, in those days all he really wanted was to encourage us to pull down our pants; he admits that now. He still sounds self-serving in *The End of Sex,* exactly like a fortyish man who has divorced one wife and is now married to a younger woman, a woman he passionately wants to keep exclusively in his bed. So he says *we*'ve had enough of free and easy sex; and what *we* need now is love. Sex has become something "we have, like dinner." He believes now the ultimate "erotic challenge" is high monogamy, which is a state of love and lust that can only be achieved in marriage.

He assures us that high monogamy does not represent a return to the repression of Victorian mores. Everyone who espouses committed sex (except Jerry Falwell and the Vatican) hastens to assure us they aren't preaching repression. This too may be true. But if it is, why has recreational sex gone underground? Why has it become something we don't admit to doing—or if we do confess to lust without love, we do so in breast-beating fashion, swearing it's disgusting, degrading, self-destructive?

No one will admit to the *fantasy* of the zipless fuck anymore. And so far, no one seems to notice the new monogamy fantasy benefits men more than women. They will have no trouble finding partners; the supply of wonderful women is endless. We, however, will have trouble. They have outgrown the vigorous lust of their youth anyway. *We haven't.*

"It's easy to see why casual sex doesn't serve men's needs anymore," Jillian says. She came of age in the 1960s, a little before sex became obligatory. "I'm glad I was old enough then to make up my own mind about what was good for me; and I still am. The same men who once told me sex was 'natural, healthy, good for you,' now say the same thing about commitment.

"Men! They have what they really wanted in the first place: sex without marriage, whenever they want it. Now they know we'll sleep with them if they dangle commitment in front of our noses. We don't demand rings like our mothers did. We'll be faithful if they want us to. If they get tired of us, they can find casual sex anyway. Men are in no way trapped, as they were twenty years ago when nice girls demanded marriage; and nice girls were in a position to make demands.

"And the big bonus is: If we aren't sleeping around so much, we don't know how good they are or how good they *aren't* in bed. The sexual revolution was bad for men in one way: We learned a lot of them simply are not good lovers."

If the experience of multiple partners taught us anything, it taught us men aren't as interested in satisfying women as we would like them to be. Kara and I have often lamented that in our hallway conversations. Our dissatisfaction with the men we've known and our increasing inability to find men our own age who are interested in us has made us more creative in our choice of partners. Like other pragmatic women, we have given up the dating criteria of our high school days. No longer does he have to be older, smarter, richer, taller. He can be younger, poorer, of a different race, far less intelligent, married, or bisexual. Kara is even entertaining the notion of sleeping with a woman. "Wouldn't it be great to find out you're bisexual?" she asks. "It would increase the options!"

Single women are still getting their, *our,* sexual needs met. As in so many other areas of American life circa the Reagan years, the values we espouse publicly are in sharp contrast to the way we lead our lives. We know it isn't fashionable to talk of affairs unless they are love affairs—so we keep quiet.

Kara has fewer casual encounters than she had in the past, but that, she says, is because "so few men appeal to me now. When I was twenty-five, they all looked good. Not so now." Her latest period of relative monogamy with Curt is prompted by expediency, not love. Curt is a black version of Tom Selleck, muscles and an adequate intellect. He is forty-two, but looks twenty-eight. "He's good, he's available." Very available—he lives in the apartment building next door.

And Curt is certainly charming: a true ladies' man. Kara isn't his only woman, a fact that doesn't bother her, except for the minor infections he gives her from time to time. He isn't her only man either, just her main man. And she has no illusions about what they are to each other. She talks about him in terms of his performance in bed. Most of the time, he is "good."

She adds, "But I have to work to get him up and keep him there.

He never gets as hard as I'd like. And he won't go down on me, though he sure takes my head and guides my mouth to his cock.

"No matter who the man is, some woman's got to worship him in bed just so he can get it up and keep it up. Curt likes it when I hold my hand around the base of his cock when he's inside me. He can go a long time. But he never thinks I might like that kind of extra attention too. If I ask for it, he pretends not to hear. Or he gives me what I want for a little while, then stops.

"Still he can go a long time; and he has a beautiful body. Sometimes he can hardly get it off. He'll go on until I'm exhausted. Then he'll just play around after I'm finished and end up jerking himself off. One night he came over and sat on the couch and masturbated. But he was mad at me. Most of the time he's good."

They seldom go anywhere, in part because he is black and she is white and this is a small town in southern Illinois, in part because that's how Curt handles his women. One Saturday night, he took her to Peaches, a record store in St. Louis, bought her some albums, and brought her back home at midnight. He left.

"He had other plans. I was furious. That certainly wasn't my idea of a Saturday night. I'd rather have been the woman who got the sex than the one who got the records. But usually he doesn't give me any real trouble."

One night he got angry, "jealous," because another man came over while he was there. He took Kara in the kitchen, yelled at her, grabbed her chin in his hands, forced her head back, squeezed her face between his fingers until it hurt.

"But he said he was really sorry afterward. He told me he wanted to get married. Now why would I want to marry him? So I could sit home alone wondering where he was and with whom? So I could hide from the world because he gets nervous if we are seen together? So I could worry about what infection he was bringing home next? No thanks."

Kara has also had younger men, an option favored by a lot of women who still are willing to play sex like tennis: for fun.

"Younger men have their drawbacks," she says. "They get crushes and send flowers and hang around on doorsteps. But they are pretty."

Joan Collins, Alexis on "Dynasty," portrays the ultimate bitch-slut; she and other movie stars have helped popularize the younger man–older woman duo. Collins in real life, and as Alexis, has bedded down with pretty young men. Mary Tyler Moore even married one. Younger men, or so we have been promised by *Cosmopolitan,* are less competitive, more supportive, less chauvinistic, than older men.

And maybe we also see in them what our male counterparts see in younger women: They focus on us, adore us, look up to us as success symbols, role models. They are status symbols. Few women who are overweight, over thirty, and underemployed attract young men, even as partners in bed briefly.

We must have earned them by developing bodies by Jane Fonda, careers according to *Working Woman.* We must have done something. Whereas older men need only be successful to attract younger women, we must have it all to appeal to young men. What we have with them is part healthy exercise, part ego fix.

I have a young lover. Predictably, we met on a professional basis; and when he found me attractive, he asked me to jog with him. He complimented my body. I told him I was thirty-eight and the mother of a seventeen-year-old son. He said he was twenty-seven, and age didn't matter. Eventually I found out he was twenty-three, and he was right: For our purposes, age doesn't matter.

He is an eager lover, not too proud to ask "What do you like?" and not so inept that he can't manage to do it well. From the first, I insisted we meet only in his apartment so my son would never be embarrassed by him. He said, "You remind me of Helen in *Garp* [*The World According to Garp* by John Irving, my favorite novel]," and I was relieved. He wasn't illiterate. Between rounds of sex, we eat pasta in elegant sauces, which he prepares, and chat about books.

My gay friend Rob, thirty-four, had an affair this summer with a nineteen-year-old. He summed up the appeal of young bodies in one sentence: "My God, Susan, they don't even have love handles; and look how much we can teach them."

As mature, successful single women we are learning what mature successful men knew a long time ago: Power is sexy. Only this time we have the power. This power, sexual and professional, frightens men our age and older, but it excites younger men.

Until recently, I resented the fact that so many fortyish men, men who could be involved with me or my friends, chose lovers and wives exclusively from the under-thirty and, preferably, under-twenty-five age group. I had a young lover, but I'd taken him out of expediency, not preference. I would have preferred a man who could remember the night Ed Sullivan introduced the Beatles to America, who didn't regard the My Lai massacre and Kent State as history lessons, who would not be embarrassed if I told him I cried and held my sleeping baby on my lap so I would not be alone while I watched Bobby Kennedy's funeral on television. When I found myself deep in a conversation about rock videos with my young lover, I thought about men my age who actually *chose* this level of exchange—and I was angry.

I thought they were responding to the allure of unwrinkled young flesh. I was wrong. They are won over by the upturned face and glowing eyes of young women who are looking for direction. A lot of twenty-four-year-olds don't have bodies as good as mine—but they have something I don't: naivete, the willingness to believe what he does is more important than what I do. They do not insist on equality. They have not yet thought even to *ask* for it.

I finally understood this over lunch with two friends, Jane and Carol. We were discussing a mutual male friend. An advertising man in his early forties who thrives on attention, he was being followed around by yet another pert blond adoring production assistant, age twenty-four. The young blonde told Carol: "I do so worry about him. He works too hard; and no one really understands him." No thirty-eight-year-old woman could even say that without giggling.

We laughed about this office romance in the way women our age do laugh about men our age: defensively, with occasional tears in our eyes. We shake our heads in disbelief at the sheer numbers of sweet young women in the world. "He's so transparent," Carol said. "Any woman but the most naive would see right through him." And so he picks the most naive.

Women really crave understanding, but men only say they do. Understanding implies love and acceptance of the bad and the good, the human qualities. My middle-aged friend only wants someone to find the good qualities and magnify them. He wants to look into eyes that are magnifying mirrors. Maybe we have made him that insecure.

Carol said, "I wish he could find an interesting woman his own age. This girl is nothing special. She's slim, but not exceptionally pretty. Not exceptionally talented. Not exceptionally bright. Not exceptionally anything."

"That is her charm," Jane said.

Successful, attractive women are better, smarter, than that. I realized we were; and I knew the contest was not between young flesh and crow's-feet. If he could find a forty-year-old woman capable of sitting through meetings, her chair next to his, but pulled slightly away from the table so she could fix her eager, earnest gaze on his profile, a forty-year-old who would follow him around, pen and pad in hand, taking notes and chirping on cue, "How brilliant, how brilliant," a woman who could sacrifice her ego to his—then he would probably be glad she remembered when the Beatles actually performed together and would choose her over the twenty-four-year-old.

I have made this discovery more slowly than many women. A lot of desperate post-thirty women are trying to compete in the twenty-four-year-old arena. They see what it is they have to do; and they are trying. Lynne is trying to be such a woman for Roger. She is prepared to change her whole life to suit him because she wants to be married. What she can't quite manage is the wide-eyed look of wonder. Occasionally her raw needs are so apparent in her eyes, I wonder how he can possibly look in there and not want to run and hide.

Thus forty-year-old men marry twenty-four-year-old women.

Jillian, who's been through several young men in the past few years, says, "We're more likely than men to bore of the adulation. We need different things from young lovers than they do. For us, the reaffirmation of our sexual appeal is most important. And from a practical standpoint, a young man in good shape can be a real sexual athlete, whereas a forty-year-old lawyer can wheeze so badly when he comes, he scares you. Men marry their young lovers, but women usually don't. Maybe that's partly social pressure, but I don't think social disapproval would scare most of us. If you're free enough about yourself to sleep with a younger man, you'd probably marry him if you wanted to. We're just smarter than that."

Jillian's is an interesting observation. *Ms.* says monogamy is in and casual sex didn't work for most of us because we can't separate the romantic and the erotic. Yet Jillian believes we can and do—much more efficiently than men our age. She says, "Women no longer marry a man because the sex works out."

For Jillian, "The sex almost always works out, but most of the men I sleep with aren't men I would ever consider marrying." The latest one is a truck driver. "He isn't stupid, but he is uncomplicated. He's very macho in that he calls me 'honey' and pats my ass. And he's so classic: When he was unemployed for a few weeks, he was impotent. The first time it happened, he was embarrassed. The second time, he said he wouldn't be back until he was sure he 'worked.'

"I didn't know if I should call him and try and be his friend or leave him alone. I finally decided: This is only sex. If the sex doesn't work, we haven't got anything else. I didn't call him. When he got another job, he came back. Everything was fine."

She defines their relationship as "something a little more than casual sex, because it's regular, even though we have no commitment.

"But don't get me wrong: I've had some great one-night stands. I don't put down casual sex like a lot of women do now. Since we all became yuppies, we've grown so serious. I compare people to city magazines. A few years ago it was trendy to be flip, to be unabashedly into consumerism and put-downs. The city mags all read the same: flip and trendy. Now we are most interested in accumulating things than ever, but we are more private about it. We don't acknowledge our lust for accumulating. And we have traded snap put-downs for serious, therapeutic analysis. Yuppies are the most serious, boring people in the world. And have you read a city magazine lately? Only *New York* is still doing it right. The others are boring.

"Yuppies want their sex the same way: serious and boring."

Like Mae West, Jillian thinks sex without love is not so bad: "I've had some good casual sex. I'm guilty of that! Guilty, guilty, guilty. Whatever we do, we're guilty. If we have good sex, we should not have enjoyed it so much; and if we have bad sex, it was our own fault.

"The only socially acceptable sex now is love sex. Okay, we don't have to be married like our mothers did. But we have to be in love. That just means they don't have to worry about supporting us."

We are still damned if we do and damned if we don't. Sluts or prudes. Men, on the other hand, are studs or romantics. "Do you really think the double standard is gone?" Jillian asks. "I don't."

I wanted a group of women to talk about the double standard; and they hedged. I met eight Chicago women, all in their thirties, at Jerome's, an outdoor café on Clark. We drank interesting wines by the glass and cappuccino. A very attractive red-headed woman at a nearby table eavesdropped on our conversation. The eight included three never marrieds, and four formerly marrieds, including three who had children. They were a journalist, two teachers—one high school, one college—a secretary, two corporate executives, one nurse, and an actress.

"I try not to think too much about the unfairness in relationships between the sexes," the journalist said, "because if I do, then I turn sour on men. And I can't afford to do that. I need them."

An executive added, "It's like the poor, you know. We try not to think too much about the bag ladies out there because then it makes us feel guilty when we hire accountants to find tax loopholes for us. The 1980s are the compromise decade for women—we are all bag ladies of a sort—but we sound like politicians when we talk about compromise—so we don't use the word."

They were, except for the actress, who may have felt her profession compelled her to be "different," united in their dislike for casual sex. "I won't sleep with anyone until I feel like he knows me too well not to *not* call back," the high school teacher said. Later she added, "I think our mothers were right after all: If we give it away, they don't value it. And we weren't getting that much out of sex with multiple partners. At least I wasn't."

Other women said they weren't either. Five of the seven said they were involved in "relationships" where the sex was mostly satisfactory.

"My only gripe," the nurse (who was not "involved") said, "is all the gay men in the world now. Every time you meet a nice sensitive guy who remembers what you said to him ten minutes ago and how you drink your coffee he turns out to be gay."

The other women agreed: The worst thing about men today is there are too few of them who are straight and single—and too many of us. Ten years ago a similar group of women would have had a laundry list of complaints about men, including complaints about their performance in bed. "Too few" would not have made the list.

The nurse said she had fallen in love with a gay male nurse, who had "encouraged" her to do so. "He wanted to try going to bed with me. He said he had gone to bed with women in the past and maybe it would work this time because he liked me so much. Well, it didn't work; and things got tense between us. Before, he had been affectionate, touching my hand or patting my arm when we worked together, putting his head in my lap when he came over to watch TV.

"After the sex, he withdrew his affection. I would have been happy just to have the affection. I felt like he was punishing me because he couldn't 'perform.' He told me I should have known all along he was gay and just wanted to be my friend. Well, that made me crazy. He certainly didn't behave like a gay in the beginning."

The story made the other women more angry than anything anyone had said. Gay men, they agreed, had a lot of hostility toward women. Or at least some gay men did: the ones who "flirted" or "led women on." Everyone knew a gay male who had. And why, they asked, were there so many gay men today?

The actress laughed and said, "Listen, there are two things professional women all have in common today: They entertain friends in restaurants, not at home, and they have at least one gay male friend."

All but one woman did have a close gay friend.

Their anger did not extend to their own friends, just to those *other* gay men who could be giving us what we need and aren't, who have chosen each other instead. They seemed to feel the same way I had felt about forty-year-old men who choose twenty-year-old women.

The journalist said, "I don't think the jury is really in on what causes homosexuality; and I'm willing to accept the biology theory to a point. But there must be some psychological components too. Maybe there are different kinds of gays. The gay men I know seem stuck in adolescence. They're teenage boys who are scared of women, scared of testing their manhood. I really believe they could get over it, get past that point, if they wanted to. They *want* to be gay."

For most of the next hour, we discussed gay men, as if this one segment of men were responsible for the current man shortage. The redhead at the nearby table continued to listen. I thought she was another writer. When the women began to leave, one by one, she approached me.

"I'd like to talk to you," she said, "for your book. I have something different to say than what you've heard here."

Kelly, twenty-nine, a flight attendant based in Houston, lives with a bisexual male. "My man sounds like the male nurse. He wanted to consummate a relationship with me long before it actually happened. We just didn't give up. He wanted to quit, but I wouldn't let him. He wanted to retreat into that safe 'I'm gay,' stance, but I knew he was a bi. He was too interested in me not to be.

"I guess this sounds crazy, but I don't care if he has male lovers. That's a different side to him, a need I can't fulfill, so why should I be jealous of it? He doesn't mind sharing me with other men either; I think he thinks the sex I have with other men is more lusty. It's more intercourse-oriented, but not more exciting. When we make love, we seldom have intercourse. We usually satisfy each other orally or manually. Other men always have to penetrate.

"I like being with him better. He is more tender, more sensual, than any man I've ever known. He nurtures me in both physical and nonphysical ways.

"The thing women have always complained most about is not getting enough foreplay. Well, with a gay lover, you get all the foreplay you want. Some of those women who are being critical of gays should try gay men."

"Maybe they would, if they could. Not all gay men are interested in women as lovers."

She said that many of her lover's gay friends were bisexual and interested in women, at least to some extent, but afraid to establish close physical ties with women because they feared failure: being unable to effect penetration.

"Gay men and straight women have a natural affinity for each other," she insisted. "Gay men love feminine things and admire the qualities in us other men hold in contempt. You were talking about the double standard. Of course there are two standards for everything, sex, money, work, everything. White straight men have one standard; and women, minorities, gays have another.

"Why do you think women are so comfortable with gay men, black men, young men, poor men? It's because we are on the same level with them. We are equal; and we are never equal with straight white men who outearn us."

Kelly was married to a "successful, white straight man." The marriage lasted less than two years. "We married when he had just finished his MBA and been hired for his first job. We were crazy for each other. Then he got to be ashamed of me. I think he suddenly realized successful men don't marry flight attendants. He wanted me to quit my job, go back to school, or donate my time to charity if I couldn't do anything else. That was ridiculous. We needed my income; and I love flying."

He wasn't, she says, a very good lover. "It was just straight fucking; he wasn't imaginative. He didn't want to loll around in bed all morning the way my lover does."

Did she see her current relationship as a compromise? Was she settling for what she could get from men?

"No, I don't think he's a compromise. Well, maybe I would be thrilled to death if we had everything we have now plus he was straight. Maybe it would, probably it would, make life easier. I grew up in an Irish Catholic family; and my brother is a monk. Sure my life would be easier in some ways if he were straight. But he's no compromise."

When I told Jillian about Kelly, she said, "Well, the one thing I haven't done and won't do is a gay or bisexual male. I'm afraid of AIDS. Besides, I feel exactly the opposite way Kelly does. I don't mind being in competition with members of my own sex, but not with men. How do you compete with sweet young *boys?*"

And Kara, for all her empathy with lesbian women, is contemptuous of gay males. "I can understand why a woman would want to be a homosexual, but not a man. Why limit yourself to the worst half of the human race?"

Lynne, who has more gay male friends than anyone I know, says "They're wonderful friends. When I go places with Bob, and I ask him if a guy is looking at me or him, he puts his hand on his hip and says, 'If you don't know, sweetie, then he's looking at me.' I love that sense of humor; I love being with him. But who needs the agony of trying to reform gays? You can't save them."

Several of Lynne's female friends are angry at gays. "I work with a female editor who hates them on principle. She is forty-one and can't get laid. I think she holds every single gay responsible."

Isn't it interesting that gay males and forty-year-old men who date twenty-year-old women get the full power of our wrath now? We don't dare get angry at the available straights who date women their age, do we?

Jillian says, "We can only afford to get mad at men who withhold sex. We haven't got anything to lose by being mad at them."

Men have withheld sex only recently. According to famed sex therapists Drs. William Masters and Virginia Johnson, loss of desire is the number-one problem in America. In their February 1984 issue, *McCall's* magazine reported that 20 percent of the U. S. population suffers from lack of desire. Refusing sex used to be a woman's ploy, a way of getting what she wanted from her man, usually her husband, or the means of punishing him for something he had or had not done. Now both men and women withhold. And the women's magazines devote pages to telling us how to pique his interest again, and ours.

The new sensitive man doesn't like being used as a sex object. He has forgotten that he used women this way before he became so sensitive.

"Men used to joke about how they wouldn't mind being sex objects," Jillian says. "No more. They hate being treated as nothing more than the satisfiers of female lust. If you're only interested in a man for sex, you can't let him know that. He wants you to tell him he's a great lover, of course, but he also wants to hear how much you love *him*.

"Isn't it funny that men have discovered romance—and marriage?"

Jillian and Kara end relationships when a man pushes for marriage. For several months Kara was seeing Mike, a divorced father who has custody of his four-year-old daughter, a nice warm modern man. He wanted to marry her. She liked him until he did.

"I'm not sure what happens to me when a man begins to care that much about me," she says. "I feel suffocated. I can't stand having someone crawl all over me. The last night we went out, we had dinner and saw a show with another couple. They were all drinking; I don't like to drink more than one drink. So I felt uncomfortable with them anyway. Then Mike couldn't take his hands off me. He was fawning all over me. I thought I was going to explode.

"He would do anything for me; and I guess I felt contemptuous of him because he would. Maybe I don't like myself very much; and I don't trust anyone who likes me, any man who wants to marry me.

"Maybe that's why I never got married."

But the sex had never been good with Mike either. "I went to bed with him because I liked him, and he was nice to me, not because I wanted to. Even at that, we'd been seeing each other for months before we had sex."

When she told him it was over, she felt "total relief."

For Kara, and for me, intimacy is physical, sexual. The boundaries we set around our emotions, private thoughts, personal lives, are the kinds of boundaries men have traditionally set. Like men, we can sleep with someone for months and never disclose our checking account balances, our feelings about our last lovers, the names of crazy relatives.

I am not always so direct at ending relationships when men begin crossing the lines I have drawn around us as a couple, around myself alone. But as soon as the lines are crossed, the ending is taking shape in my head.

When I was a little girl—less than six, I wasn't in school yet—we had a plague of caterpillars one summer. I stole matches from the kitchen drawer. In those days my mother lit the gas stove every time she used a burner. I took the matches outside under the big oak tree that was most full of caterpillars. Fat fuzzy worms plopped regularly to the ground. It was also a dry summer. I drew lines in the dust with a stick from the tree and placed caterpillars in their quadrant, a good distance from the center line. The caterpillars who crawled away in the other direction were spared; the ones who crawled past the line toward me were burned as soon as they crossed the line. My mother caught me before too many caterpillars went up in flames.

As a woman, I am still drawing lines in the dirt. I remember now that the tips of my little-girl fingers were burned ever so slightly in the immolation process; and I suppose they still are being burned, but I don't notice anymore.

Maybe choosing to be single is choosing the barely perceptible burn on the tips of one's fingers over the major trial by fire one is sure to endure in marriage. Ending a love affair hurts, but not as much as beginning a marriage. When the sex is no longer very good, ending seems like the thing to do.

But ironically, my most lasting postdivorce relationship was ended by him, not me—and not because the sex stopped being very good.

When I met Ryan in the late 1970s, he was married but separated, an elusive man who drank too much, still looked like the sixties political radical he had been, held strong and controversial opinions about politics, literature, and sex, projected an appealing air of the cynical renegade—and was impossible to take in anything but small doses. He was my own myth made flesh: the perfect no-strings (zipless) fuck.

For four years he drifted in and out of my apartment, my bed, my life. The sex was the kind of experience one reads about in letters to *Penthouse*. He was an oral genius.

Then he decided he was an alcoholic, joined Alcoholics Anonymous, and became, in the words of a therapist I consulted about our problems, "an AA junkie." A man who specializes in treating the spouses and loved ones of alcoholics, this therapist said our relationship had followed a classic pattern. I stayed with him when he drank. We broke up when he stopped.

I could manage his drinking, or so I thought. When he was drunk, I threw him out of bed, made him dress and leave. He returned in a few days repentant and horny. I knew how much more he was probably drinking alone in his room, but I didn't worry about it, any more than I worried about his wife and three children living on the other side of town. Worrying about each other wasn't part of the agreement between us.

Sex was the basis of our relationship. I didn't call him when the car broke down, when editors didn't send my checks on time.

Then his wife finally divorced him; and he lost his job. He made AA and God the new anchors in his life and said that if I couldn't "change" with him, we couldn't stay together.

"I tried to find salvation in politics, drugs, booze, sex. None of them worked," he said. "They were all just places to hide out. I've found it now; and it's more important than anything, even sex."

I didn't believe him. I didn't believe any man would walk away from the kind of sex we had. We broke up, went back together again, broke up. He called the sexual bond an "obsession"; and toward the end, he cried out in painful resentment when he came.

He wanted me to join Al-Anon, the support group for families of alcoholics. I attended a few meetings and listened to women tell stories about learning to cope with men who were still drinking, who beat them, who, drunk or sober, were absolutely obsessed with self. Those tired women, crazy lights shining in their eyes, scared me. "Wife" was burned on their foreheads in angry red letters. They talked about love and tolerance, patience, kindness, and God; and I didn't want to be like them.

He wanted me to change my life and follow him. When we broke up for the last time, he said, "I don't ever expect the sex to be any better than it is between us. Sex is just not enough."

That shocked me. I hadn't expected to hear a man say, "Sex is not enough."

Six months later he was married to a woman who had thrown herself into Al-Anon, who was willing to "share" his new life.

"Why," Jillian asks, "when a man says he wants you to share his life does he not realize the word *share* implies a mutual give and take, a commingling of two lives? Why does he assume the two of you will share one life—*his?*"

Maybe because we assume it.

"I'm tired of doing everything myself," Lynne says. *"I want someone to take care of me for a change. I want a big dramatic change in my life; and that's only going to happen with marriage. Yes, I'm fitting into his life; and he isn't fitting into mine. But I don't care. I like his life.*

"Sex is a priority, but not the highest priority now. I've had sex. We've all had sex. Isn't it time for something else. Well, isn't it?"

By the early 1980s celibacy, or talking about celibacy, had become trendy. A book and several magazine articles encouraged us to say no. The new celibacy was supposed to be the thinking person's response to the sex overload in our culture.

It was now acceptable to talk about the lean periods between lovers, which everyone must surely have experienced before it was acceptable.

Lynne, who does not miss participating in cultural trends says, she "took six months off from sex" in the past year.

Although she was never too involved in her career for sex, as some women have been, she was, during this period, too involved with improving herself.

"I had just broken up with Mike. I was dieting and in group therapy. It seemed important to concentrate on fixing me, on getting everything worked out so the next time, the next man, would be right. I was relieved and relaxed knowing this was a period when I wasn't going to worry about getting laid.

"I didn't miss sex because I knew it would be waiting for me when I got my life together. I couldn't get what I wanted for me until I got better. I knew the quality of my relationships would improve when I was in better shape, mentally and physically.

"When I came out of it, I knew I had put aside the destructive habits. And from now on sex would be part of an integrated relationship, a relationship that gave me what I wanted to have."

Lynne "feels sorry" for women who "think they have to have sex all the time in their lives to be happy."

Kara and I have met with such disapproving pity from other women. We feel like leftovers from the sexual revolution. While other women are mouthing euphemisms from the "other things are more important" school of thought, we are, Kara says, "still hung up on cock." When I hear other women describe the other things that are more important, I still think our hang-up makes more sense.

Colleen, thirty, never married, Catholic public relations executive, has been "in love" with Ken, thirty-five, a divorced producer of TV commercials, for four years. This is a typical 1980s relationship: It's serious, or she is serious, and sex is secondary.

Ken's interest in sex peaks in the spring and wanes in the fall. Winters are definitely the frigid season. "I'm not particularly looking forward to another winter with Ken," Colleen admits. "He has almost no sex drive in the winter. We have sex very seldom. When we do have it, he comes too fast because it's been such a long time."

She thinks if they lived together the sex would improve. "If we slept together every night, I'm sure we would have sex more often. I've heard married women say they have sex three times a week; and that's almost unbelievable to me. I can't imagine having sex that often. I'd love to try."

But Ken doesn't want to live with Colleen.

She says, "He has a hard time with intimacy. He just doesn't know how to trust, because his wife cheated on him. He didn't want the divorce (which was six years ago), so I think it's hard for him to trust." But she hopes he will "trust" again and someday be able to develop a warm and loving relationship; and she hopes she will be the one he trusts. He's given her no reason to believe she will be. He isn't meeting her needs, sexual or emotional, yet she fights to keep "the relationship" together.

And she doesn't believe in casual sex, even in the winter. "You have to know someone before sex is good," she says. "The first few times with someone new, sex is so awkward and uncomfortable. You have to get past that stage before sex is good."

This is almost an article of faith with women now: Sex can't be good at first, because "it" has to develop slowly.

Maybe her reluctance to experiment, to suffer that initial discomfort with someone new, helps keep Colleen in Ken's bed—just as a decade ago our belief in better sex "out there somewhere" inspired us to leave our boring beds.

Sex isn't the impetus for change it was then. Virginity isn't a liability anymore either.

"I don't know if there are more virgins past the age of twenty than there used to be, but it's more acceptable to remain a virgin past twenty now. But people do find it strange if you're past twenty-five and a virgin," Shelly says.

At twenty-eight, she says, "I'm saving myself for marriage, for the right man, the one I will love the rest of my life. I know that sounds trite and corny and old-fashioned, but it's what I want. And I believe I'll get what I want. It will happen for me."

Shelly could become one of the new breed, the terminally single woman, never marrieds between the ages of thirty-five and fifty. The longer she waits for sex and marriage, the higher her expectations of each and her standards for her future husband climb. She believes her parents had a "perfect" marriage; and she is holding out for the same thing. Her Mr. Wonderful is a fantasy man. She isn't the first woman to invent a man when real ones disappointed.

A friend who laments Shelly's virgin state says, "What she needs is someone wonderful, someone to sweep her off her feet."

Without realizing it, this friend has defined the terminally single woman: a woman who clings to impossible ideals of romance while waiting to be swept off her feet by the mythical knight.

How much longer will Shelly wait for sex and/or marriage?

A junior lawyer in a large firm of corporate lawyers, Shelly frequently works evenings and weekends. If one of her clients has a crisis, she puts her personal life aside to meet the crisis. One weekend she had out-of-town guests and a client who needed her. The guests looked after themselves.

She expects as much of herself as she does of a man: perfection. She works out regularly; and her body is lithe, trim, shapely. Her hair is shiny and beautifully cut, tinted a fragile shade of honey blond. Her violets bloom exuberantly. Her clothes, business suit preppy, are always correct. No missing buttons, mud-splattered pantyhose, sagging hems.

How could she settle for less in a man?

"I am in love," she says, "with a man I've been seeing off and on for four years. We break up, but we always get back together. He'll call me in the middle of the night after I haven't seen him for weeks or months. He'll come over and spend hours talking to me, then disappear again. The emotional connection between us is strong, but I guess he isn't ready to make the kind of commitment I want."

How could she love someone for four years, without having sex?

"I'm just determined to wait for marriage," she says.

Her friend believes this man cannot be "the one." She says, "If he were, it would have happened by now. He would have carried her off to bed. They would have been overcome with desire for each other."

This friend also fears that when Shelly finally makes love, she is "bound to be disappointed. How could anything live up to what she must be expecting by now? I can't imagine her wedding night. I'm afraid it will be a disaster."

A decade ago we were sexually optimistic: We were sure that good sex was out there waiting for us, if we only went in search of it. No matter how many times we were disappointed in bed, we believed the next time would be good. Finally we realized men were getting the best deal in sexual freedom. And we were getting quantity, but not quality.

Today we are romantically optimistic: We're sure the sex will be wonderful if only we fall in love. We have gone almost full circle. In the forties and fifties our mothers also believed in the power of love to move the earth beneath their beds. Will we make it all the way back to square one: to the place where we have to worry about our reputations if we "sleep around"?

Not surprisingly, Shelly wants a marriage like her mother's. "My parents were in love with each other to the end," she says. "My father died a few years ago; and my mother will never get over him. It's so hard for her, for both of us, being without him. He was a wonderful person.

"I want to find someone just as wonderful."

Does she expect him to be a virgin? Is the man she loves now a virgin?

"No, I'm sure he isn't. And no, I don't expect my husband to be. It would be nice if he were. But I might as well be realistic about that, don't you think?"

Shelly says the difference between her and other single women she knows—women who do have sexual relationships—is "they're willing to settle and I'm not. I don't blame them. It's not a moral issue. I don't think I'm any better than they are. But I do think I value myself more, have higher standards. I won't give myself away cheaply. ✓

"It has nothing to do with religion. I was raised in a very lenient Protestant home. I went to Sunday school at the Presbyterian church because it was within walking distance of our home. Sometimes my parents went to church, but religion wasn't the focus of their lives.

"So, I'm not Catholic or anything. It's not that."

Her friends think Shelly hangs on to the myth of her "relationship" with this man because the myth keeps her safe. She doesn't have to risk a real involvement with a man who might expect her to go to bed with him. 'Nothing will ever match her illusions of her parents' perfect marriage," one friend says. "This distant love protects her illusions."

Shelly says, "My parents' marriage wasn't an illusion; it was as close to perfect as two people can come. But my friends may be right: Nothing in my life may ever match what they had."

She adds, "If I weren't a virgin, they wouldn't be so critical of me." Virginity may be more acceptable than it was ten years ago, but it's still extraordinary. Shelly tells few people. And I understand why. When I told Kara about Shelly, she asked, "Is she a lesbian?"

"There are really only two kinds of women who don't want to get laid: virgins and lesbians. Any virgin older than eighteen is probably a lesbian," said a forty-year-old engineer I'd known for ten minutes in a cowboy bar. We were pushed together in the crowd at Bobby's in Fairview Heights, Illinois. He was wearing jeans, plaid shirt, boots, but he wouldn't have fooled anyone into believing he'd ever had a comfortable moment on a horse. People between eighteen and fifty-plus go to Bobby's for the loud music, the food, served twenty-four hours a day, and most important, to meet each other.

In front of us, a bleached blond woman, at least forty-five, dressed in tight jeans, high heels, and a glittery blue shirt, shifted her weight from one foot to the other in time with the music, emphasizing each beat with an exaggerated sway of her bony hips. He pointed to her and mouthed, "Desperate."

A battle of the bands was being waged that night: Three country-and-western groups played in turn; the customers voted for their favorite. I went with a friend only because he manages one of the bands and needed my vote. When the engineer tried to pick me up, I told him I was only there to vote. He shrugged his shoulders and made his observation about women. He apparently didn't think I was a virgin. My friend came over then and put his arm around me. The engineer said, "You should have told me you were taken."

Most single women who have lived alone for any length of time, without forming a visible attachment to a man, have been accused or suspected of being a lesbian, usually by a man she doesn't want. Most of us cringe and rush to deny the charge. Some of us will even go to bed with a man to prove we're straight.

Joyce is a lesbian—and a virgin.

"You probably don't know many thirty-year-old virgins," she says. "Most lesbian women have been with men; and a lot have been married and have children. Maybe they knew they were lesbians all along, but they hoped they weren't. They hoped sex with men would change them. Or maybe they just didn't know what they were and thought sex was supposed to be awful. Either way, they had sex with men, not out of desire, but because that's what society expected them to do."

Joyce lives in Fairview Heights, a conservative community that is home to many military personnel and their families stationed at nearby Scott Air Force Base. She says, "There is a real underground lesbian community on the east side [of the St. Louis area], but straights don't know it exists. We blend in. Women can be room-mates without people suspecting they are lovers. Women earn so little money, rooming together makes financial sense. And lesbians are less active in this part of the country than gay males. We're afraid of getting raped if we come out. So we keep to ourselves."

Many of Joyce's lesbian friends live as couples; they consider themselves "married." Joyce describes these women as "nest build-ers."

She says, "They are so cozy, they might as well be straight couples. They complain because they can't be legally married and get tax benefits. I guess it's okay, but it's not what I want. Also, whenever a woman I sleep with gets too close to me, I back away. I don't want everybody trying to figure out which one I am, the butch or la femme. I don't want to be labeled; and I don't like being close.

"You know how it is when you've been with a man a while and he thinks he owns you, he puts his hands on you in public and orders your food or drinks for you because he knows what you want. Well, lesbian women can be the same way about each other. When a woman starts expecting me to be with her—and crying if I'm not—and making cow eyes at me in public, I split."

Joyce dated men until she was twenty-three. "I couldn't stand to have them touch me or kiss me. Obviously I never dated any guy for long, but I still didn't see that I was a lesbian. A man told me I was frigid; and I believed him. I needed to be in love to have sex with a man, I thought. Isn't that what we're supposed to think?

"Then I realized I was in love. There was someone I wanted to touch; and she was a woman.

"The first morning I woke up in bed with a woman I was horrified at what I'd done. She had long red hair and it was spread out around her head on the pillow. She was lying on her stomach. The curve of her back was so feminine, so sweet. I looked at her back; and I wanted to kiss it. And I kept saying the word to myself: *lesbian*.

"That's what I am: a pervert, a sick person, a lesbian."

Joyce has stopped thinking of herself as perverted and sick. Now she believes she is merely different, forever an outsider in the straight world. When she is with straight friends, she sometimes feels like a fraud.

"If they don't know, it bothers me, but some people just can't know. They couldn't handle it. Even people who know I'm lesbian don't want to hear any details. They can talk about sex with a man in graphic detail, but they are politely revolted if I say anything about a woman's breasts.

"And I have a teaching job in a junior college, so I have to be careful. How many parents would want me teaching their eighteen- and nineteen-year-olds?"

At twenty-three, Joyce realized she'd never be able to have children of her own, "but I don't think I wanted them anyway. I'm not responsible for myself sometimes, so how can I be responsible for kids? I'm not sure I even understand maternal love. Some of my friends have little kids; I don't know how they stand them.

"But I do think about growing old and not having any kids or grandkids. I'm an only child. I had a brother, but he was killed in an automobile accident when we were in high school. So there's only me and my parents. When they're gone, I won't have anyone. No link to my past. No one to visit me in the nursing home."

Her parents live in Colorado; she visits several times a year. She is very close to her father, with whom she shares athletic abilities and interests. "I don't like my mom much. I feel sorry for her. She's so typical of women in her generation. She's had face-lifts, a tummy tuck, and a boob job. She's terrified of getting old. Whenever she goes through another operation, I want to say to her, 'Don't do it. You don't have to do it anymore. Dad will still love you.' Maybe she's really not doing it for him anymore; maybe it's all for her.

"She reeks of Estee Lauder all the time. Her hair is still perfectly blond, perfectly sprayed in place. She goes to club meetings and does things for the community. I shouldn't put her down; she does some good. But that's purely a by-product. She's out there to show off her pretty face, her size-four body. If she knew the truth about me—the real reason I'm not married 'yet'—she would die."

Joyce isn't going to tell her parents either. She doesn't have to come out at home, she says, because unlike her nest-building friends, she has no one to drag along on family visits. "They would get suspicious if I brought home a woman friend and we shared a bed, wouldn't they?"

When Joyce begins a relationship she knows it isn't going to last. "I never expect to have a long relationship. Sometimes I juggle two or three people. I have a good straight friend who tells me I'm still in adolescence. She believes we all have homosexual tendencies in adolescence, but we grow up and outgrow them.

"And she says I haven't."

Joyce resents the "immature" label, which she says is applied to lesbians as often as "perverted" is. A therapist friend, a woman who is also a lesbian, says the "immature" label derives from the straight person's bias about sex: If it isn't intercourse, it isn't sex.

She says, "What everyone really wants to know is: How do lesbians do it? Men are especially titillated by the question. Men have this fantasy that lesbians would stop making love to each other and both pounce greedily on any male who climbed in their bed. They are turned on by the idea of two women making love because they imagine themselves in the middle, because they really can't imagine two women making love.

"How can two people make love without one cock? They assume one must play the 'male,' strap on a dildo and act tough, while the other plays 'female.' "

John Sayles's critically acclaimed 1983 movie *Lianna,* the sensitive portrayal of one woman's journey into homosexuality, perpetuated the stereotype. Warm, soft, female (and married) Lianna was seduced by Ruth, the older woman who was tough, cool, and trench-coated.

Joyce laughs at these characterizations. "I guess straights think one woman plays a man because they can't see sex working any other way. They have limited erotic imaginations. Even gay males are remarkably obtuse about what lesbians do and are to each other. One gay male friend asked me if I could still consider myself a virgin since I'd surely been penetrated by dildoes. When I told him I hadn't been, he was shocked. He asked, 'How can you have sex all those years without some kind of penetration ever taking place?' "

Everyone who has a lesbian friend has heard this line: Only a woman really knows how to satisfy a woman. Joyce swears that's true, though she's never been to bed with a man and has no real basis for comparison. "To be honest," she says, "I've never had sex that was really outstanding either. Maybe most people don't."

Joyce, like most lesbian women, considers herself a feminist. In the early days of the movement, we straight feminists were more willing to identify with our lesbian sisters. Now many of us feel the women's movement lost ground because of its identification with lesbian issues and abortion rights. And Joyce says, "Straights, feminist or not, don't want to be too closely associated with our issues. Gay rights are a hot potato in the conservative period we're in now.

"But you straights are wrong in turning away from us. We have more in common with you than you do with men. Equality isn't here yet. I think a lot of women are scared now, scared and huddling next to men for protection. They'll have to learn all over again the price they pay for that bit of protection.

"Besides," she laughs, "if there aren't enough men to go around, aren't we going to become exactly like women in prisons who turn to each other for physical release?"

5

The Evolving Singles Scene

*I meet hundreds of men [says Lucy]. We drink wine, we
exchange personal stories, go in the Jacuzzi and go to bed
and maybe it lasts a week or two.*
                    from *Friends of the Opposite Sex* (1984)
                              by Sara Davidson

Think of the singles scene as the arena in which unattached men
and women make sexual connections. When making these connections is a top priority, as it was in the 1960s and early
1970s, the arena is expansive. When sexual pleasure becomes sub-
ordinated to other concerns—the finding of a marital partner, a
parent for one's future child—the arena narrows. The meeting ground
is a serious place where rules are clearly defined.

In the late 1960s any place men and women happened to be
together was a pick-up place. The scene was fluid, casual. Mick
Jagger cried, "I can't get no satisfaction," and we all understood
the meaning. Nothing was more important than getting it.

Everyone was young then; most of us were students. Wearing
long hair and short skirts, we cared about rock music and politics
and sex. And why not? We had grown up watching "American
Bandstand" and the funeral of an assassinated president on television. Men our age were everywhere.

Jillian says, "What I remember about the years from 1966 to
1969 is the line guys used. It was always a variation of, 'Take off
your clothes because it's the right thing to do.' Did anyone ever say
no in the late 1960s? I went to so many parties at Mizzou [University
of Missouri at Columbia]. We passed around jugs of Gallo hearty

burgundy wine and joints. And I seldom went home alone from one of those parties, if I went home, that is.

"We found corners to fuck in then. We weren't supposed to have inhibitions; and so we didn't. Inhibitions were something our parents had. We didn't. The wine and the pot helped, but there was also a great sense of political duty about our sex. People who marched in antiwar demonstrations would be at the same parties together later that night. If you hadn't been arrested, you had something to celebrate. If you had been arrested, and were out on bond your parents had wired to you, well, you had something to celebrate too.

"We felt close, united in our opposition to the war. The sex often came out of that feeling. To refuse to fuck was to compromise your participation in the movement."

Even if the sex wasn't very good, and it often wasn't for women, we kept taking down our pants and opening our legs on request. How could we not? Articles were being written about us; we were changing the moral character of our times. We were the first generation to flaunt sexual conventions en masse. The headiness of being who we were influenced many of us to experiment sexually with men we didn't know—or really want to know.

Jillian was on the fringes of an SDS group at Mizzou. "I was never an organizer, only a follower. But I was involved enough to be caught up in the spirit of the group. And sex and rock were integral components of that spirit. One of my classmates met her husband on the protest line. A cop knocked him down; and he fell at her feet.

"That was romance, sixties style. We wore little makeup, no frills, and no bras. We were seductive in a way women hadn't been before. It was so blatant, yet not artificial or contrived."

The amenities of courtship were eliminated. Men didn't have to woo us with flowers and dinners. They only had to remind us, "Sex is good for you." Sex was supposed to make us free, but there was no true equality in the sexual revolution—or in the antiwar movement.

Jillian recalls the movement men were always "in charge."

She says, "Women did pretty much what they were told to do. It's no surprise that a lot of the women who were most active in the movement became feminists and lesbians. They had to be mad as hell at the men who pushed them around. They ran mimeograph machines and made coffee. Sexually, they were passed around from one man to another. The seriously political people professed to believe commitments were bourgeois. You were supposed to have sex with anyone without forming ties. Even if a couple really cared about each other, they felt obligated to behave promiscuously.

"You were supposed to pursue your lusts then, not ignore them. The result of that was a lot of women got passed around."

Less political women also felt the pressures of "free" sex.

Kara, who sympathized with the antiwar movement without being too involved, recalls, "In those days we went to bed with whoever asked us. Refusing seemed impolite. I did a lot of drugs then, so the sex wasn't memorable certainly. It wasn't important. I just did it.

"Drugs influenced attitudes about sex in the 1960s. They helped melt down inhibitions. A lot of us wouldn't have done the things we did had we been stone cold sober."

If coupling was easy in the 1960s, so was uncoupling. We developed a new behavioral code for breaking up: no grudges. By the time the sixties ended, we had come to think of ourselves as people who could do almost anything, who were entitled to almost everything, who had and always would have an abundance of choices ahead. We'd ended a war and changed the country's attitudes about sex. Why should we settle for early marriage, early motherhood, as our mothers had? Would any woman who was young in the late 1960s, when even a plain woman had her choice of bed mates, ever have believed that the early 1980s would find bright and beautiful women desperately searching for a suitable mate? Of course not.

The great legacy of the sixties was not sexual freedom. The legacy was the tremendous sense we had of unlimited options. We did not have to choose.

In the 1960s we didn't need singles bars or any formalized system of meeting each other, because so many of us were in the same places at the same time. The 1970s were different. We were out of school and working. No great political cause united us. For the first time in our lives, men and women began to have trouble finding each other.

Disco was invented as an excuse to bring us together, though not too close together. In the 1970s we were becoming a little more selective about sex, but no more interested in long-term commitments. It was the me decade, not the we decade.

After I was divorced in 1976, I sporadically did the local disco scene with friends. We went in groups of three or four women, danced with men, sometimes exchanged kisses with them on the dance floor or the parking lot. And that was it. We usually left early with headaches and red eyes from the noise and smoke. I know *one* woman who met her second husband at a disco. The rest of us never made a date. We could have; we just didn't.

"That's because a lot of the men were married," Jillian reminds me. "The cute ones."

We had a foolproof method for picking out the married ones: When a man asked for our phone numbers, we would ask for his before we gave him ours. Inevitably a married man would say, "I don't have a phone." We met an inordinate number of men in the late 1970s who claimed to be corporate executives, doctors, airline pilots—and did not own telephones.

Toward the end of our disco days, my married friend Janet ran into one of the "pilots" at a company Christmas party she attended with her husband: The pilot, accompanied by his wife, the mother of his four children, was actually a medical technician. Jillian and I came to regard him as our male symbol of the disco era: a total fraud who could dance well.

Colleen worked as a waitress at a Kansas City disco in the late 1970s. She says, "It was an awful job. I didn't mind the short tight outfits or all the men in white suits, gold chains, and hair perms. But the floor was so crowded. You could count on dropping or dumping a tray of drinks every other night. And the tips were bad. After several months, I was lucky and got transferred to the piano bar. The crowd was older, quieter; and they tipped."

She did see pick-ups being made in the disco, but "mostly I saw the same people all the time. I think if you had gone around to every big disco in Kansas City, you would have seen the same 200 people every weekend. Yeah, they picked each other up sometimes, but mostly they just exchanged lines."

By the end of the seventies disco was dead. Singles bars were in. Never mind the excuse of the dance. We didn't need the BeeGees singing "How Deep Is Your Love." The appeal of singles bars was as blatant as tie-dyed shirts over unfettered breasts. But it was less wholesome. We weren't so young anymore; and the edges were hardened by incipient desperation.

Lynne says, "Is there a woman over twenty-five who can't remember going into a bar and being approached by a guy who asked her what her sign was and told her she was too nice to be there? No wonder nobody got married in the late seventies. Everybody eventually went into one of those bars; and everybody hated them."

Jillian remembers the middle-aged man who told her the story of his life, right up to the point of finding his wife in bed with another man, at which point he began to cry. She says, "There were some snatches of very real, very sad conversations in those places. They were always between people who didn't intend to leave with each other. As long as you could keep up the ships-passing-in-the-night image, you could be honest. Otherwise, no."

The middle-aged man patted Jillian's hand, thanked her for listening to him, and told her she had too much "class" for a bar. He expressed an attitude typical of men who went to the bars, hit on women, took them home if they could—and secretly believed the women who went home with strangers they met in bars were not very classy.

Men in bars were older versions of the high school boys they had been in the back seats of cars. Their object was to score. If they didn't, they were disappointed; and if they did, they were disappointed too.

By the early 1980s singles were placing ads in the classifieds that read, "Tired of the bar scene. Want to find love and commitment."

Women had decided the bar scene didn't work for them; men had reached the same conclusion. We were all looking for serious relationships. Baby boomers, male and female, were beginning to feel a new kind of job frustration. We had thought our success was limited only by our desire to achieve, our willingness to work hard. We were beginning to discover success was also limited by our sheer numbers. So many of us, so many bright, educated, talented, promotable people, were fighting for the same few jobs at the top. We began to regard each other as a place where some of our expectations for happiness could be met.

The single scene in the 1980s reflects our new seriousness of purpose. We are no longer looking for suitable sexual partners, people we can discard in the morning.

Men want the advantages of a two-career life-style, the succor a wife can provide, children. Women want everything their mothers had—marriage, babies, suburban homes; and we want those husbands to share the housework. We want marriage and careers, babies and terrific figures. We continue to think every single one of us is going to have it all in spite of the odds.

But we do realize that time is running out.

We are meeting each other at health clubs, through video dating services, and classified ads. Our criteria for men has become increasingly selective even as the available man pool shrinks. It makes no sense; some of us are bound to be disappointed.

We are finding men by hounding our friends, coworkers, and relatives to fix us up. We are doing the things Ann Landers and Abigail Van Buren have been suggesting for years: We are joining groups that attract men, donating our time to the charities they serve. In the 1970s we pursued our interests; in the 1980s we pursue theirs. We are willing to change to get them—if we deem them worth having.

Finally we are taking the advice of our mothers and *Seventeen* magazine: "Find out what he likes and pretend you like it too." I never was very good at feigning interest, but only lately has it cost me the company of certain men.

We are pursuing men, husbands, as actively as we have pursued careers. And sex is not nearly as important as it once was. We are a lot more interested in the questions relating to long-term compatibility. Singles ads clearly state smoking or nonsmoking preferences, as if we were booking seats on airplanes. I know a woman who refused to go out with a dark sexy commodities broker because he voted Republican.

Lynne tried a video dating service exclusively for Jews. "But all the men I met were dorks. They were interested in things like keeping a kosher kitchen. I'm not that religious. I don't feel that Jewish. I'm willing to change a lot."

She isn't willing to date dorks and nerds, no matter how fine they may be inside. And no underachievers either.

"I want a man who is earning a good living," she says. "Someone who hasn't got time to hang out in bars."

She met Roger at a private party in the home of a friend. Lynne disdains the classifieds. "The men have to be creeps," she says.

Several of her friends who have placed or answered ads say she is right. One says, "I placed an ad and heard from three men who would go to bed with any woman who wasn't overweight, one who was looking for a Christian wife, and two who were much older, very shy, newly divorced, and afraid to go out looking.

"They were creeps or losers."

Yet magazine articles, including a piece in the August 1983 issue of Ms., tell us love through the classifieds is possible. "Maybe if you don't have very high expectations," another woman says. "If you want a very ordinary, very boring guy who is very specific about what he wants from you, I guess you can find it."

The eighties meeting place—health clubs—is limited to the trim and fit. People who meet this way must be willing to build relationships slowly, the way they build muscles. Jillian, who was a member of Vic Tanny long before it was fashionable, says, "In the past few years, I have seen couples get together at the club. They usually eye each other up for days before conversation gets to the how-many-reps can-you-do-on-that-machine point. And I haven't seen anyone who does not look good in a leotard leave with a male escort."

Yet again the magazines tell us we can meet men in health clubs even if we're not in great shape. Again and again, magazine articles on where to find the men make it sound like the men really are out there if you just know where to look. Jillian says, "They leave out important pieces of information when they're compiling their lists of tips. For instance, a lot of the guys who hang out at health clubs are gay. In fact, the guys who take aerobics classes are all gay. If you doubt me, go watch them. They're watching each other's asses, not ours."

I work out at home alone; and I don't go to bars either. I count on my work to put men in my path; it usually does. Kara says we might have better luck with men if we went in search of them instead of waiting for them t appear. "We end up with the men who just happen to be there," she says. "Maybe we should be more active in recruiting them."

Maybe we should. But we probably won't, because we don't know where to look. When I go out with women friends now, we are not looking for men to flirt with, dance with, kiss, as we were back in the disco days. We aren't approached by men when we sit together in bars, pubs, bistros, restaurants. Men have learned that women in pairs or groups are really out to talk with each other about our jobs, kids, lives—not to be picked up. They respect our public privacy in a way they didn't ten years ago when women unaccompanied by men were all fair game.

Besides, male friends tell me, they don't have to approach us anymore. We go after them in public places. A very attractive Los Angeles attorney in his late twenties says he only goes to crowded night spots with a date, because "the women hit on you in such numbers it's almost scary." He has been approached by women more than once in the brief span of time in which his date left him alone to go to the ladies room.

Apparently this is a common problem. A woman (late twenties) I met at the hairstylist told this story: "I was with a date at Lucius Boomer's [a night spot on the Landing]. I left him for about ten minutes to go to the john. When I came back some gorgeous woman was hanging on him. 'Thanks,' I said to him. 'I leave for ten minutes and you hit on someone else.' 'I didn't,' he insisted. 'She's hitting on me.' Smiling, she kept hanging on to his arm. Finally I unlinked her arm from his and told her, 'Look, he's with me. You'll have to find someone who isn't on a date.' "

No wonder women can go out in groups alone without being pestered by men anymore. We no longer expect them to make advances. If once we got our ego fix by collecting propositions, now we get it by counting admiring glances.

On a typical night out with women friends, we dress for seductions that are never going to take place; and we know it.

It was one of those early crisp fall nights in St. Louis when Kara and I went with two friends to the Central West End. We were celebrating the forthcoming marriage of the youngest one, Julie, twenty-three. Rather, we were putting her through the premarital hazing process: telling her all the reasons she really shouldn't marry.

We wandered from place to place, eating chicken wings at Culpepper's, crab Rangoon at Tavern on the Plaza, drinking margaritas at the Flamingo. We walked down the cobblestone streets of Maryland Plaza, climbed on the fountain, and followed its concrete edge, one behind another. We knew we looked hot: four women in tight jeans, two blondes, one redhead, one brunette—the essence of choice in hair color, breast size, length of leg. We knew the men on dates sitting on benches with their women were smiling and thinking the same kinds of thoughts dieters have in pastry shops. We enjoyed their admiration; and that's really all we wanted from them. We are not the sort of women who would go home with strangers anyway.

In the 1960s we measured our allure by the number of men who asked us to bed, in the 1970s by the number of men who asked us out. And now we measure our appeal alone by checking the rearview in the mirrors of fitting rooms, the reflection in the mirrored walls of health clubs as we dance and twist in leotards. We can estimate the level of lust in the eyes of the men we meet. And we don't need them to tell us when we look good anymore, because we know.

The dance is more demanding than it ever was. It's done alone while Olivia Newton-John sings "Physical." We wear sweat bands; and we really sweat. Unlike the go-go girls who danced in cages, we don't dance for an audience.

Men do now. Male strippers wouldn't have been a phenomenon twenty years ago, ten years ago. Today they are. Groups of women go to clubs where beautiful young men strip down to satin jock straps. We scream and cheer, leer and stomp and whistle, and stash dollar bills inside those jock straps. Yes, women threw their hotel room keys on the stage when Tom Jones sang, but there was only one Tom Jones. Male strippers are everywhere.

Kara and I went with a group to P.T.'s, a club on the outskirts of East St. Louis, Illinois, with a group of women who were celebrating the promotion of one woman. At P.T.'s, women strip five nights a week. On Ladies Night, only men strip. Saturdays, women are the main show and men strip in a smaller back room.

We went on Ladies Night, Tuesday, when male patrons are not allowed into the club at all. A bouncer explained: "The rumor is the strippers are all fags; and a lot of queers would hang out here on Ladies Night if they could get in. It would turn the place into one of those clubs for cross-dressers."

Are the strippers gay? "Nah," he said. "A couple of them are married. If any of them are queers, I don't know about it."

The women don't seem to care. They love the strippers. Each one has his own act, a persona defined by costume and special effects. The Count is carried on stage in a coffin, leaps out wearing a black cape and suit. Smoke from dry ice billows around him.

"You can't tell the married women from the single women here," a waitress said. "They all get into the mood. I think it takes the place of sex for all of them. If you've been married a while, you need something to make the sex interesting again. You need fantasy. So you can get it here. You can get all hot and go home to Harry and get it off. If you're not married, the fantasy is here too. You can enjoy it, then go home and get yourself off."

Or do it in the johns. When Kara came back from the rest room, she whispered, "You're not going to believe this—a woman was masturbating in the stall next to me."

I laughed. Later it didn't seem so funny. I don't want to go back to P.T.'s.

6

Marriage and Kids: Where We Have Been

"I want my wife back!" Martin Harris.
"I want my life back!" Norma Jean Harris.
       —from *Norma Jean the Termite Queen* (1975)
                 by Sheila Ballantyne

Such was the state of marriage in the 1970s, between women struggling to achieve a greater degree of personal freedom and men struggling to maintain the status quo. Yet none of my married suburban friends, good Edwardsville Catholic mothers all, understood Sheila Ballantyne's book. Norma Jean was my favorite character in those how-to-get-out-of-a-bad-marriage novels written in the 1970s. She was witty in the self-deprecating manner of fictional housewives and on the brink of emotional collapse. Her kids were horrid, not cute. Her husband, who didn't know the kids very well, persisted in thinking they were cute and *she* was horrid.

I pushed Norma Jean on friend after friend and waited hopefully for their responses. They were always disappointing. My friends didn't know why Norma Jean was so unhappy—or they wouldn't admit they did. And I was often angry at them because they were so determinedly, patently dense. It was the year they were making Christmas wreaths from computer cards spray-painted red and green; and one of them held a cookie exchange. I had my husband and the husband of a friend, one of *their* husbands, make my twelve dozen apricot balls the night before the cookie party while I typed a short story. The women were shocked, mildly amused, titillated even. *How* did I get two men to make apricot balls, they wanted to know.

64

Didn't they see what a rip-off marriage was for women? Couldn't they understand men were living real lives and we were making it possible for them to do so by running their suits to the cleaners, cooking their meals, raising their kids, cleaning their toilet bowls, baking their goddam cookies? Obviously they couldn't. The seeds of discord between women who stayed at home and those who didn't were sown in such afternoons as the one we spent passing plastic baggies full of cookies back and forth. We didn't understand each other anymore. And we were losing touch with our common ground, the playground in the park where we had met when our kids were very small and we all still believed we were doing something important; and it was the same thing.

They stayed married; and I got divorced.

Later some of these women divorced too, but their divorces were not like mine. For them divorce was a way station to be inhabited as briefly as possible. They quickly exchanged one man for another. In fact, they seldom decided to leave the first husband until the second seemed firmly on the line. They finished the last dance with partner number one as they whirled right into the next with number two. It wasn't marriage that displeased them; it was merely *one* man.

Sometimes I felt so superior to them. Sometimes I envied them so much.

They said they were not feminists; and I said I was. The women's movement had two central messages. I (and other formerly marrieds) bought one of them: *No woman need stay in an oppressive marriage picking up someone else's socks.* Never marrieds bought the other message: *Postpone marriage and motherhood and build a solid career, so that you will never have to stay home picking up socks.* We had discovered traditional marriage and motherhood did not work to our advantage. We believed when we finally married (or remarried) we would remake marriage so it did work for us.

"I can always get married," single career women joked when it was hard to pay the bills, but they weren't kidding. They thought they could "always" get married; and they thought they would. There was no hurry. Wasn't late motherhood chic?

I remember a January 1980 conversation with Lynne and Carla, another friend, in the now defunct Brandy's in the Central West End. We were eating chicken livers beneath dying plants; and I was trying to figure out if the marks across the gay waiter's chest (exposed by his unbuttoned shirt) really were made by a whip when Lynne said, "I can always have a baby at forty." She had said it before. This particular conversation was no different than many I'd been hearing since the early 1970s, but for the first time I found myself as angry at my never married friends as I had once been at suburban wives.

Couldn't they see they were buying into a myth, perpetuating a fraud no less dangerous than the feminine mystique? Didn't they understand they were selling out their sisters and themselves with their position: "*I* can make marriage work even though *you* couldn't; *I* can have children without disrupting my life even though *you* couldn't."

Lynne, who was a few years away from thirty, said there was absolutely no reason to rush into marriage and motherhood; and Carla, already thirty-four, agreed. Yet marry and mother they eventually would because they planned to have it all, happiness via the feminist mystique. Of course they would not compromise careers or give up tennis lessons or lose their figures. They spouted the avant-garde theory of parenting: It's the quality of time not the quantity that counts. Women, like Lynne and Carla, who had never raised children knew this better than any of us.

Their attitude, a mix of arrogance and naivete, irritated me. They sounded like high school kids maintaining one really did not have to turn thirty if one chose not. I wanted to say, as Peter Pan says to the audience when Tinkerbell, the fairy, is dying: "If you believe in fairies, clap your hands." But I was sure they would have.

Never marrieds eagerly accepted the new wisdom: Motherhood could and should be deferred into one's thirties. They talked as if one could as easily decide to have a baby at forty as cosmetic surgery around the eyes. And baby, of course, would pop out of the magic opening just as easily—and be perfect, even as an infant smart enough to thrive on quality time. (Though married now, at thirty-nine, Carla still hasn't had her baby. She's been to a fertility specialist who finally advised her to try adoption, and to adoption agencies who have told her she will be too "old" when her name finally reaches the top of the list.)

The 1970s were a decade of biological optimism, a time when our choices, or so we thought, were limited only by our vision. In January 1980, Lynne and Carla still believed.

Women in general were angry in the 1970s, but married women were the angriest. We had our own fiction genre: the unhappily-married-and-mad-about-it novel. *The Women's Room* (1977), by Marilyn French, is perhaps the best known. Certainly its male characters are some of the most insensitive and exploitative in print. Unmarried women who read those books must have found encouragement for their holding position.

Single women had career guidebooks and *Cosmopolitan* to tell them how to get laid, more money for clothes, and no day-care worries. They seemed to be having all the fun in bed; they had the career jump on the rest of us.

Married women had husbands who wouldn't help with the housework and didn't want them to go back to work anyway. We were being told that it was possible for women to have it all just as men have always done. We looked at our lives; and saw we didn't. Single women, on the other hand, still had every reason to believe they *would*. Their lives held glamor and promise.

There was no reason to marry and every reason to get out of a marriage.

The life-style pages of newspapers (newly renamed from the "women's pages") ran stories about women who had walked out on their husbands and children in search of themselves. These women went back to school and became lawyers or gynecologists. They took young men into their beds. Or slept with women. They wrote books and made lots of money. We didn't hear how their husbands and children coped with the wake left by their passage. That was another story, which we got a few years later. At the time we read only about the women, their motives and their guilts, their sorrows and their joys. They were cultural heroines. For a brief time in the 1970s we applauded women who threw up their hands and walked away.

I almost became one of those women, but I didn't *quite* have the guts. I couldn't *quite* convince myself my son would be just as well off without me as those women in the stories had. Maybe I didn't leave, but I often felt like leaving. I hated being a housewife; and my anger at the role permeated every corner of my life.

Jane O'Reilly, writing in the first issue of *Ms.*, spring 1972, defined the housewife's moment of truth: the shock of recognition she felt when she knew she had been had—by marriage, by men, by society, by other women, her mother, and herself. The realization would occur while she was in the process of doing her usual chores or being her usual self-effacing womanly self. Or when someone, usually a man, would say something inane, such as "How about something to eat?" to a weekend hostess who had just finished cleaning up after her third major meal of the day. This moment of discovery was followed by a "Click!"—the verbal equivalent of the old cartoon light bulb turning on overhead—as everything fell into place for her and she began, mentally at least, packing her bags.

Click! came to stand for the moment of truth; and women by the score wrote their Click! letters to *Ms.*

My own Click! occurred in the spring of 1972 before I had read *Ms.* and had a definition for what happened to me as I walked down the stairs carrying a basket of laundry. I looked down to avoid tripping over the bottom step and discovered my thumb firmly imbedded in my husband's piss-stained underwear. Something inside me went over the wall. Click! *No* adult human should have to do this for another adult able-bodied human. No intelligent woman should consider marital servitude her life's work.

This new realization, coupled with my increasing awareness that sex in marriage, in *my* marriage, was never going to make the earth move, left me ripe for the message shortly to be delivered in my first copy of *Ms.* magazine. Yes, Click! I was ready.

I was so ready for change, I even briefly considered running away with the impotent Wisconsin poet. Actually, it was "running away," the topic of articles, that I found attractive, romantic—not the poet. But how to get free of a "good" husband determined to keep me—and his son, his family—intact? I could leave the son as hostage to my fate, couldn't I?

Richard was and is a wonderful father; and he made more money than I did. Turning custody over to him made sense. My new feminist soul rebelled against being paid off: I didn't want alimony, a large settlement, child support. I couldn't keep the house without his help; and I didn't want his help. Besides, leaving everything in place would assuage my guilt.

So I ran, flew, to Wisconsin one weekend. Richard asked Barb, my best friend, to shorten Richie's new pants. When I talked to her on the phone, she said she was shortening Richie's pants; and we both cried. And I came back home.

Tearfully, she had told me, "You'll never be happy with yourself if you leave Richie." And she was right. I returned home chastened. And it took me four more years to get a divorce. For most of those four years, I wasn't trying to be a wife anymore, not really; I was there for my son. I was there because I was still too cowardly to live the feminist rhetoric I spouted. While playing at independence, I had the safety net of my marriage, the security of knowing I was supposed to fail anyway.

I carried my husband's underwear down the stairs into the laundry room without ever telling him how I felt about doing his laundry, about ironing his shirts before my blouses, about being second. How much I hated being second! I talked to my friends about that, but not to him, not until it was too late. And he didn't understand anyway.

I was also there because he begged me not to leave and I didn't know how to refuse him. I remember thinking in those days I'd never be a writer until I led an honest life; and I didn't know how to lead an honest life and be married too.

"What do you want?" he yelled. "What can I do to make you happy?"

I didn't want anything he could give me. I wanted choices; and staying with him limited them.

Jessica, thirty-six, a midwestern executive, did walk away from her husband and her kids, but she did it in the early 1980s, years after the "wife who walked" was a heroine. It was no longer really the thing to do.

Jessica's Click!—her moment of 1970s truth—was more dramatic than mine, though it didn't lead her to immediate divorce either. A good Catholic mother of two, she was the kind of woman for whom women's magazines were published each month. She baked cookies and kept her toenails painted, built snowmen for her kids and banked fires for her husband. Tall, slim, long-legged, and sensual, Jessica dresses in ruffles and lace, short straight skirts, all the acoutrements of femininity. She wears her hair long and curled and looks exactly like what she is: a man's woman.

"When my husband wasn't happy," she says, "I knew it was either my fault, or if it wasn't my fault, I could fix it anyway. I took responsibility for his happiness as he took physical responsibility for me. And I did everything I could to make him happy. I really tried to be the perfect wife and mother.

"When he still wasn't happy, I went to a psychologist to find out what was wrong with *me*. I was seeing this psychologist every week when I learned my husband was having an affair. I had been blaming myself for not making him happy; and he was unhappy because he was guilty about cheating on me."

The psychologist, a male, had never suggested that some of her husband's unhappiness might be *his* responsibility.

Jessica learned about the affair from a friend, then called her husband at the office and asked if it were true. He admitted his indiscretion and promised "to end it." She packed a suitcase and left the kids at home with her mother looking after them, a note on the table for him. She told him she was going away for a weekend to think things over.

The weekend lasted two weeks.

"I was going to visit a friend in Colorado, but I got tired of driving. I checked into a ski lodge for one night, or so I thought. Then I met this man. We had the most incredible sex. It was wonderful the first time, like you read about in books. So I stayed on at the lodge. He had a two-week vacation; and I spent the two weeks with him, using my husband's credit cards to finance my half of the trip. I called home regularly to talk to the kids, but I wouldn't tell my husband where I was or when I was coming back."

After two weeks, she went back home—and stayed there for several years, but she was never the same sweet, accommodating wife again.

"I didn't care if he was happy or not anymore. I decided it was my turn to do something for myself. I went back to school, earned my bachelor's and my master's degrees. When I wanted to, I stayed out late. I took my own life back. He didn't like it; he didn't understand it. But there was nothing he could do about it.

"When he had that affair—and he was genuinely sorry afterward—he changed things between us. I couldn't feel the same way about the marriage. It was marred. He tried to make things work after that. Really, he did. He wanted to make me happy, but he couldn't anymore. I didn't want anything from him."

Jessica finally left in 1982. She left all of them, not just him. "I decided it was his turn to be the parent. I had done everything for the kids all those years. I had been the perfect mother. I was the kind of mother who took the kids driving on Sunday afternoon in search of adventure. We followed fire trucks to fires. We took nature hikes; and I could tell them about the animals and plants we saw from reading books I'd checked out of the library.

"I did everything. My cookies were never even burned around the edges. Well, it was his turn to give. My turn to take care of me."

Before the 1970s, women did not think in terms of "turns." It was always our turn to parent, their turn to earn money. Marriage provided us with the only real security we had; and mothering was an important element in that security. My mother told me when I was a child that my eldest sister, who had no children, was "not in a good position." Mother's implication was that Ellen, like a barren queen, could be abandoned, and justifiably so, if her husband desired.

The women's movement changed our lives. We were supposed to work, but they were also expected to parent. Traditional marriage, which was designed to accommodate *their* needs more than ours, couldn't function properly without a full-time wife-mother at home. We wanted out of those stuffy arrangements—or we wanted not to enter into them. We politicized housework and cared passionately about who did the dishes—because *we* did, of course. But we thought other marriages, more egalitarian unions, were in our futures. *Someday.*

Never married women, if they looked at our dissolving marriages at all, looked at them with pitying contempt. We only served as bad examples, negative statistics to encourage them to set their standards ever higher.

"I knew the way my married friends were married wasn't the way to do it," Jillian says. "When they told me they were unhappy, I always asked them why they quit their jobs—which was dumb. Would their low-paying, low-status jobs have made them happy?"

Jillian thought then, when she was younger than thirty, that marriage was possibly, probably, in her future too. So did Kara: "The only thing I knew about marriage was I wouldn't make the same mistakes other women did. I didn't have a lot of career ambition, so it wasn't a career I was sure I would maintain after marriage. It was my independence. I knew I wouldn't stop being myself. I could see these women had changed—and not for the better; and I didn't know why."

Jillian and Kara both watched their friends make changes for men. Kara says, "I had roommates who turned into different people when they started dating the guys they eventually married. They became sweet, accommodating, dependent. They cleaned up the apartment; they learned how to cook.

"When Mary Kay, my last roommate, was ready to marry George, it felt like a huge barrier was thrown up between us. The last few months we lived together, we weren't close. I'm sure she knew how I felt about marriage by then; and so she felt defensive around me. Maybe my attitude implied criticism of her choice.

"There was only one time in those last weeks we lived together when I felt we were close. She had lost her diamond engagement ring; she was crawling around the floor searching for it and whimpering. I was asleep, but I heard her whimpering, though I'm usually hard to wake up. I helped her look for the ring and found it for her. She was really happy with me for a while."

Jillian and Kara are, by their own admission, not overachievers. They have jobs, not careers: Kara works as a job counselor for the county earning $17,000 a year; Jillian is the office manager for a small plumbing parts distributor and earns $20,000 annually. They haven't avoided marriage in favor of work.

Lynne *is* a high achiever. Yet she too says her career didn't keep her from getting married in he twenties. She earns $35,000-plus, depending on how hard she works. He accounts include a national fast food chain's breakfast advertising. She is really good at her work, labeled by many in the field as one of the top five advertising copywriters in St. Louis—but when she's seriously in love she works less.

"I was just in no hurry to settle down to one man in my twenties," she says. "I didn't make a conscious choice to achieve success first. None of my friends was getting married either. Everyone was working, traveling, having a good time. And I was caught up in that whole thing. In my twenties, I knew so many men. And I didn't see any point in settling down with one of them. Why pick one when there would be more?

"I didn't want kids yet either. I had both my abortions in my late twenties; and I don't regret them. There were a lot of other things I had to do. It wasn't that I minded the idea of being a single mother. I just wasn't ready yet for kids.

"And I saw no reason to rush, when I had so much time."

The few women Lynne did know who married young, women from her high school class, daughters of her mother's friends, "were the type who wore frayed maternity tops in their third pregnancy in four years. I would run into them in Schnuck's [a grocery] and not have anything to say to them. I knew their life wasn't going to be mine. They seemed so old, so much older than I felt I was."

Remaining single, childless, for as long as possible permitted never marrieds to cling to their youth for an unprecedented length of time. Thirty became the adult milestone twenty-one had been. At thirty, one "grew up." We baby boomers were the first generation that didn't automatically accept the yoke of adult responsibility—marriage, parenthood, the two-car garage—as soon as we'd finished our formal educations. We went to school longer than any other generation had. And when we'd finished school, we still weren't quite ready to grow up. We wanted Europe before we bought baby shoes.

"I wanted to work hard and play hard," Lynne says. "I wanted to see places I'd never seen, do drugs and drink too much. And I knew I couldn't do those things when I became somebody's mother."

"There were men I could have married," Jillian says, "but I wasn't ready to draw boxes around my days yet."

And Kara admits, "I just couldn't force myself to make a choice. I was still young as long as I didn't make a choice. I still had time to make *any* choice. As soon as I picked someone, then my life was set; and I was afraid I'd never be able to change it again."

They didn't have the same attitude toward babies their mothers must have had at their age: Jillian and Kara didn't stand cooing over the cradles of friends' babies. "When friends had babies, we stopped being close," Jillian says. "Nothing comes between a friendship like motherhood."

But for all their indifference to marriage and motherhood in the 1970s, never marrieds planned to marry and mother eventually. No one figured the odds in advance and warned them the supply of potential husbands would be slim when they looked for a mate. No one said, "On the basis of statistical probability, you're going to end up alone."

Like Harriet Vane, mystery writer Dorothy Sayers's fictional heroine, they believed marriage was a "surrender"—and they weren't yet ready to surrender. Plucky Harriet succumbed to Lord Peter Wimsey, an erudite, sophisticated feminist, in one of literature's wittiest courtships. Then they had one of the mushiest honeymoons in print.

It was exactly the fate never marrieds were sure happily awaited them as soon as they were tired of being single.

Formerly marrieds blamed one man for their unhappiness in marriage. Never marrieds blamed us for making the wrong sorts of marriages. All of us thought *we,* the next time, the first time, would do it differently—right. We didn't see patterns; we didn't analyze numbers.

Surely we could not have imagined asking each other the great question of the 1980s: "Where are all the men for women like us?"

7

Marriage and Kids: Where We Are Now

EXECUTIVE WEDDINGS ... HOW TO FIND THE TIME.
—cover blurb, *Working Woman*, June 1984

MARRYING LATE ... WHY WOMEN FINALLY SAY YES.
—cover blurb, *Ms.*, March 1981

POSTPARTUM AMBITION: HOW A BABY CAN BOOST YOUR CAREER.
—cover blurb, *Working Woman*, January 1985

When Mary Cunningham wed Bill Agee, the love-struck stars of the Bendix story made the corporate world safe for marriage again.

Cunningham, whose fifteen-month rise to top management at Bendix, guided by mentor Agee, led to her resignation under fire, is a fairy-tale princess for the 1980s. Blond and bright, pure of heart and loyal to a fault, she really only wanted to have it all: corporate power and a seat to the right of her man's throne. Her story combines love and work, which made it irresistible to women; and it has the requisite happy ending—marriage.

It's a sign of the times that few people, feminists included, asked the right questions about the Bendix scandal. When Cunningham was hired in June 1979, fresh from a Harvard MBA program, by then-president Agee, both were married—to other people. She took the job, which started at $21,000 less than another offer, and moved from New York to Detroit, a city her husband hated, because: "He [Agee] needs my help. Investment banking firms want someone with my credentials; but Agee needs me" (from *Powerplay: What Really*

Happened at Bendix, by Mary Cunningham with Fran Schumer). Apparently he did. Soon his lone confidante, she was quickly promoted to vice-president.

Not surprisingly, suggestions of improper behavior were made. Agee announced publicly that "nothing [was] going on" between him and his chief aide-de-camp, who also happened to be his very good personal and family friend. Hounded by the press, Cunningham soon resigned. Phil Donahue and Gloria Steinem were sympathetic to her plight, that of a self-described victim of sexism.

Cunningham's credentials (presumably impeccable) and her chastity (who cares?) were beside the point. Why had she sacrificed her career to a man?

Ten years ago we would have been furious at Cunningham for letting us all down. Today we grow misty-eyed at the thought of this corporate princess marching down the aisle trailing orange blossoms behind her. In 1981 didn't we all watch Lady Diana become Diana, Princess of Wales, in her televised wedding—and sigh with envy?

Many never married women who are approaching thirty, and those who are well into their thirties, are beginning to panic. Magazine and newspaper articles aren't delivering the same unabashed good-news medical stories they printed a decade ago when later childbirth was much heralded as safe, sane, fashionable. Now researchers warn about increased risks of infertility in the thirties, higher incidences of birth defects, and greater odds of stillbirth. The number of cesarean births has reached unprecedented levels in this country.

Now women are being warned that their biological time clocks are running down. And a lot of them are not so biologically optimistic anymore. Motherhood at forty and beyond is beginning to sound like another thing Ursula Andress can pull off more easily than most of us.

Formerly married women may already have their babies, but they have also discovered they have other problems: collecting unpaid child support, finding affordable day care, combining sex lives with single parenthood, finding a man with whom to have a sex life in the first place. Their ex-husbands have remarried to young working women and are part of the two-career couple boom, those superspenders—and *they* have become part of the nouveau poor class, the fastest growing class of poor in America: unmarried women and their dependent children. (Some economists and government statisticians predict that by the end of this century the poor will be almost entirely composed of this group.)

Their children don't have Nikes; they have reluctant stepmothers who think they don't need Nikes. Many of the formerly married women who were so angry in their first marriages are wishing themselves settled in second ones. Many formerly married, formerly middle-class women have told me, "I am tired of being poor."

All of us, formerly marrieds and never marrieds, are finding careers have not and probably will not provide all the emotional fulfillment we once thought they would. And certainly they aren't paying enough. The press touts the accomplishments and salaries of the few; the many earn far less. We thought we didn't need marriage to support us, but it turns out most of us still do, especially if we are or plan to be mothers, which it turns out most of us still do.

Our magazines tout the combo of the 1980s: business and babies. We *should* have both. *Working Woman* magazine, the executive woman's bible, is beginning to look like *Redbook* in a business suit. A maternity business suit.

Leading celebrity members of the postponing generation have married or had babies or both in the 1980s. In 1980, Marlo Thomas then forty-one, wed Phil Donahue (her first marriage); and Jane Pauley (then thirty) married Garry Trudeau (thirty-two), first time for both. In 1983, Pauley gave birth to twins, following two publicly lamented miscarriages. In 1984, Farrah Fawcett (thirty-seven) announced her first pregnancy by Ryan O'Neal, and Amy Irving disclosed hers by Steven Spielberg.

Baby lust has swept the country. Fifty-five million viewers watched Krystal Carrington (played by Linda Evans), the good queen of "Dynasty," give birth to baby Krystina. Millions more bought *People* magazine the next week with Krystal and Krystina on the cover— and read forty-two-year-old Evans's admission that she still hasn't given up on finding marriage and having a baby!

Well, baby boomers were ripe for baby lust. Their hormones at last are willing out.

Pauley, who once told an interviewer she wasn't sure if she ever wanted a husband and children, said after her marriage, "There comes a time when you realize that there are other impulses [beyond work] and it's very sad if we can't publicly admit that there is a personal, nurturing, domestic side to us. For a while we couldn't."

These glamorous role models have encouraged us to change our attitude toward marriage.

Marlo Thomas said (in the March 1981 issue of *Ms.* magazine) that she was finally ready to marry after forty-one years of being single because "the world had changed"—and because she had. Her old definition of marriage, "a negative, skinny, little space into which I would never be able to squeeze myself and all my aspirations," had been expanded to a "wide positive space that was generous and roomy enough to hold everything we wanted, including each other."

If the leaders of the movement were marching down aisles, could successful Everywoman be far behind?

In June 1984, *Working Woman* assured us, "These achieving professional women [executive brides] are not so much returning to a tradition of the past as they are transforming a tradition."

"Married" and "mother" now sound as chic and brave as "single" did ten years ago. Are these women "transforming" traditions or have they capitulated to biology and economy, to changing public tastes and social mores? Could marriage be so desirable again because the supply of marriageable men is so limited, making a husband, like flawless diamonds and sable, something *everyone* can't have?

Jillian and Kara have made up their minds: They will never marry, never mother. But they are in the minority. Dr. Joyce Brothers says her research indicates an astonishing 95 percent of single women want to be married. Shrewdly capitalizing on the statistics and spirit of the times, she has written a book telling women how to hold on to their husbands.

Single women are also willing to make a great many concessions to keep their men—as Brothers tells their married sisters to do. A decade ago these same women would have been questioning whether or not *they* wanted marriage, not worrying about what they had to do to get or keep men married. They would not have been asking what they could do for their men—but rather what their men could do for them.

Times have changed; and so have women.

Lynne knows she is making most of the concessions in her relationship with Roger, but she says, "That's how it has to be. It's never fifty-fifty." Why not? "It started out that way, didn't it?" And marrying him (or someone) is her New Year's resolution.

But, she insists, she is "dealing with limits [she] can handle." He is a busy man, so she comes to him. When he comes home from a hard day of being a lawyer and a candidate for office, he likes to find her waiting at his apartment. Ideally, he likes to find her in his bed, because he seldom gets home before midnight. But she's usually fully dressed reading on the couch.

"I'm willing to be at his place at 11:30, but not warming up his side of the bed in my nightie. I want him to talk a while before we get in bed and fall asleep. He isn't totally satisfied with that. And I think I have come a long way, probably thanks to therapy. In the past, if a man wanted me in his bed warming it up, I would have been there."

Now she is on the couch; and she feels like she has reached a new plateau in assertiveness.

What intrigues and impresses me—and sometimes infuriates me—about Lynne is her ability to believe each time: *This man is special, this man is different, this time I will get what I want.* I have sat with her through the postmortems following many relationships when she has finally admitted they stood her up, knocked her down, took from her and gave little in return. Like too many other single women, she has shared her stories of spending too much money and time on men who have spent too little time and money on her. (I have contributed those stories to the collected verses too.) But while she is in love, before it all falls apart, she gives. And she believes.

"I think happiness in love is possible," Lynne says. "I don't want to be alone. I want to try. At least, if things don't work out, I can say I gave it my all."

The day she said this she admitted quite casually that Roger had stood her up the week before. "He was busy. I can see how it happened. Men don't fit into our lives. We fit into theirs."

Other single women, even if they aren't as candid as Lynne, are also fitting themselves into the lives of men. Are they preparing for, hoping for marriage?

Colleen says, "I spend the night at his house; he doesn't spend the night at my apartment. He let me know early on that he didn't like staying at my place. The bed wasn't big enough. He has a king-size bed. And he doesn't like getting up in the morning and discovering he doesn't have the right clothes with him or something he needs to take to work is at his place, not mine.

"He said he would be sleeping at home; and I was welcome to come back there with him if I wanted. So we stay there."

Colleen thinks he needs her, or at least he needs someone. "He doesn't like to be alone. If I'm not out there by eight, he will call and ask me when I'm coming. He usually has lots of company. He has a group of single male friends who drink too much and occasionally throw up. They're younger than he is, because the men his age are married. I keep hoping he'll realize that.

"But he likes me to be there, even if we're not alone, even if we don't have sex."

Jillian says the "accommodating pattern" begins in high school. "It did for me. I got a B on my senior English composition final because I spent all my time writing my boyfriend's paper. He got an A. You know how we are at first in a relationship: We'll do anything to win their love. We knock ourselves out earning their love. At least as I got older, the crazy time got shorter."

But Colleen has been seeing Ken for four years; and the accommodating pattern looks like a holding pattern.

She wants to marry him, though it is difficult for people who care about her to understand why. Invariably described by friends, coworkers, clients as "sweet," Colleen *does* look like the kind of woman who should draw a solicitous man: Her round face is surrounded by shoulder-length soft brown hair, her big brown eyes are trusting. Ken seems as cool, closed, and detached as she is warm, open, and caring. She says, "I know someone will eventually break through his reserves. I want to be the one."

Recently Colleen introduced her friend Jessica to another friend, Eric. "It was practically love at first sight," Colleen says. "They are crazy about each other. I want to have that with Ken."

Jessica and Eric sometimes take Colleen out to dinner on Friday nights. Ken seldom takes her out. When they are together, they usually "hang around" his house, cooking meals, doing the laundry, watching television.

Jessica says, "Ken is a jerk. Eric and I ran into him at a neighborhood bar a few weeks ago. He grabbed us, said he had to talk, and took us outside to his car to share a joint. Well, he didn't talk. He unloaded on us. He said he and Colleen were 'on the skids'; and he wanted to break up, but he didn't know how to tell her. Eric was furious; we both were. Some girl got into the car, in the front seat next to him, looked at him, and said, 'Oh, you're talking about Colleen.'

"We went back inside the bar. When Ken came back in, Eric said he wanted to tell him something. But there were people hanging around so it had to wait. Eric never did get to tell him: We don't want to be responsible for passing his message to Colleen. We felt like we had been set up to do just that. We hate to see her hurt, but we can't deliver the message. I'm sure he plans to let things drift from bad to worse, to keep on pushing her in his passive-aggressive way until she gets tired and walks. He hasn't got the guts to break it off."

He will have to push much harder. The same weekend, Colleen described her relationship with Ken as "improving." Two weeks before, they'd had a fight because she told him she wanted to live with him—and he said, "Why should we live together when we'll only break up in six months?"

She interpreted his remark to mean he was afraid to trust, not to mean he didn't love her enough to live with her.

Why do women rationalize so wildly? We can be very analytical about the behavior and comments of another woman's lover. Do we want to hang onto the man in our lives so badly we'll ignore everything but a GET LOST sign on the pillow? Are they *that* precious?

Colleen says, "I want to get married. I want to have kids. Someday I think Ken will want that; and I hope I'm here when he does."

But she says she won't be waiting long past thirty. "I think about being a single mother. I love Ken and I hope things are settled between us by the time I'm thirty. If they're not, I'm not sure how much longer I will be able to wait.

"I wonder if he'd be very angry if I got pregnant?"

While Colleen contemplates single motherhood, she isn't ready yet to give up on the whole package: husband, babies, suburban house. She is more biologically pragmatic than Lynne was five years ago. Thirty, not forty or thirty-five, is her cut-off point.

Apparently many women are reaching the same conclusion.

The out-of-wedlock baby boom is apparent to anyone who reads newspapers and magazines. In 1980 (the last year for which statistics are available), out-of-wedlock births rose by 11.4 percent. The increase was largely due to the rising figure for white unwed mothers: a 17.6 percent increase.

In "Mommy Only: The Rise of the Middle-Class Unwed Mother" (June 6, 1983), *New York* magazine documented the trend. These single mothers by choice are largely women who are over thirty, well educated, and well employed. Single moms are the new cultural heroines, surpassing the runaway moms of the 1970s.

The articulate moms interviewed by *New York* talked about the "primordial" urge to reproduce—which is something they had to do for themselves, to fulfill their own needs. The motives haven't changed. Runaway moms told interviewers: It was something they had to do for themselves, to fulfill their own needs. Only the method of fulfillment is different. Babies are the 1980s answer.

And nobody has told single moms that Superwoman is dead. They do it all: herbal tea pregnancies, Lamaze classes, night feedings, and board meetings again in three weeks.

Jillian's friend Gerri, thirty-six, is part of this trend. A social agency director in Wisconsin, Gerri says her WASP family roots have been traced on both sides in elaborate family trees, linking her to a signer of the Declaration of Independence and Martha Washington's dressmaker.

"My son, Sean, is the only twig coming from a single branch in either family tree. On my dad's side my cousin, who serves as keeper of the records, called to ask me how she was supposed to enter Sean. I told her, 'Draw a straight line down from me.' Surely there have been other illegitimate births in all the generations of two families, but I suppose they were not recorded as such. Maybe the babies were given up for adoption to sterile aunts or something. I know another cousin had an abortion last year.

"Anyway, Sean is a first. The other relatives might be shocked by him, but my parents are delighted."

At thirty-four, Gerri decided she couldn't wait any longer. "I hadn't had a date in a year; and I felt like I was standing by while my fertility ebbed away. Every month when I got my period, I cried. So I just decided to find a suitable father for my child, get pregnant, and take care of the baby alone. Why not? I've always gotten everything I really wanted—by working hard for it, by doing it myself—and I *wanted* a baby.

"The man I chose was married and still is. He doesn't know he fathered Sean. It was a brief affair, deliberately initiated by me for the purpose of conception. I picked him because I knew him to be intelligent and healthy. He looked the way I would like a boy to look. Well, Sean doesn't look like him at all; he looks like my father's side of the family. But it doesn't matter; I know he has good genes. That's what I wanted. I could have done artificial insemination, of course. Two of the women in my support group [for unwed mothers] did. But I want Sean to have the option of finding his father when he's grown. By then, this man might be glad to have fathered a son."

Gerri earns $38,000 a year, so she can afford a child. She lives close to her family, who act as back-up when the sitter doesn't come. "I never have to worry about what will happen to us if I'm sick and can't work. My parents have a huge house. They are not rich, but they are comfortable. They could take us if they had to.

"But when I read about young girls keeping their babies, it makes me sad. I think they're unduly influenced by women like Farrah Fawcett. And I don't think being a single parent is the answer unless you are past thirty and well situated in the world. You need money to raise a child. Love is not enough."

Gerri's sister and brother-in-law, in their early thirties, have agreed to be Sean's guardians if anything happens to Gerri. "I've covered all the bases," she says. "It wasn't the impulsive decision of a lonely woman. Well, at least it wasn't impulsive."

Jillian says single motherhood is the only unconventional thing Gerri has ever done: "She was a cheerleader and still looks like one: blond, WASP, cheerful. She didn't do drugs or go out with the wrong guys. Gerri is the daughter of my mother's oldest friend; and all my life I've heard how Gerri came along and did things right, after I had messed up. This shocked the hell out of my mother."

Gerri "almost" got married twice. The first time, in the early 1970s, she decided she, then in her early twenties, was simply too young for commitment. "Now I think I should have grabbed him. I could have had two or three children by now. I would have liked more children. There will only be Sean because I am too old to try again. One is enough to raise alone. I don't want to put more pressure on my family or myself. I'm lucky Sean is healthy and his birth was easy."

The second time she "almost" married, Gerri was thirty.

"I was going to marry a lawyer—older, divorced, a friend of my brother-in-law. And I was going to marry him out of sheer biological panic. He realized that and called the wedding off.

"I cried and begged him to marry me. I want you to know this embarrasses me now more than anything I've done in my life. After the wedding plans were canceled, I was relieved he hadn't given in. We would have been miserable together; it's lucky one of us was smart enough to see that."

Jillian remembers the second broken engagement. "Invitations had been sent. Gerri personally called everyone and explained the wedding was off because they had cold feet. She sounded so calm, I thought she was the one who had backed out. A year later I saw her at my mother's; and she told me what had happened. At first I was surprised and disappointed that she would humble herself to an overweight, balding man. When I thought about it, I understood what had happened to her. She was desperate for a baby, not a husband."

Jillian believes Gerri would have made whatever concessions were necessary then, at age thirty, when she was so desperate to have a child. "Maybe I am willing to give in less to men because I don't have the overwhelming urge to mother. Baby lust can make you as blind as sexual lust, can't it?"

She won't "change [her] life around" to suit a man as Lynne and Colleen do. Nor will Kara: "I'd feel silly carrying my blow dryer and jeans across town. If a man sleeps with me, he sleeps here."

Jessica laughs off minor inconveniences. "One day I had to wear my jacket in the office all day because my black bra showed through my pink blouse. I always forget to take another bra with me; and the day before I'd worn a black dress. Aren't those the things you do when you're involved with someone? Eric's cats need him at home he says."

Since Jessica's children live with their father, she is free to spend her nights with Eric. Early in the relationship he asked her why she had "abandoned" her children. "That hurt," she says. "I expected him to understand. Now I think he does."

After they had been seeing each other for a few months, Jessica's daughter, Dawn, moved into her apartment. Dawn, who had been battling anorexia and bulimia since her parents' divorce, was having difficulty getting along with her father. So was Jessica. "He kept calling to talk about Dawn's problems; and I thought they were better. I thought we had the anorexia cured because she was at a normal weight. I told her she was welcome to stay with me, but she shouldn't expect me to change my life completely because she was there. I would still be spending nights with Eric a lot."

Dawn resented Eric's new place in Jessica's life; and Eric thought Jessica was too lenient with Dawn, whom he regarded as a "spoiled brat"—or so he told Colleen. Then Jessica discovered boxes of laxatives hidden in the trunk of Dawn's car and empty packages of ice cream and Sara Lee brownies in the trash. She knew the binge-purge syndrome was not cured. The week before Christmas, Dawn's behavior became so erratic she had to be admitted to a hospital care unit.

Jessica and Dawn's father were not allowed to visit, only to call or send cards, so Jessica and Eric spent a long weekend together in Chicago. "There was no reason to stay home," she says. "And we needed the time together. We had been arguing about my kids; and we didn't talk about them the whole weekend."

Dawn's hospitalization has brought them "closer." Eric is more understanding of Dawn's illness, more supportive of Jessica. But he still says, "*Our* children won't be raised like yours."

Eric does want at least one child. Jessica says, "I know this is part of the package with him. If I marry Eric, I will have to have a baby, probably soon because of my age. I never thought I wanted another child, but now I'm beginning to consider it. Eric will want me to stay home for a few years with it, then go back to work. He hasn't considered what two years could do to my career at this point. Does he think they'll hold my job?"

Unlike many women her age, Jessica isn't sterilized. (Sterilization is now the number-one method of birth control in America.) She still takes the pill. "I've never had any problems with it," she says. "My husband and I talked about sterilization after our son was born, when we knew we didn't want more children—but we never got around to doing anything.

"Maybe I really hadn't given up on the idea of more kids."

Yet Jessica says she is not really making *all* the compromises. "If we do get married, Eric will have to adjust to my kids too. It is a lot to ask of a man."

What does marriage give women to make them willing to pay such a big price: loss of freedom, middle-age motherhood, the traumas of stepfamily adjustments?

"Security," Jillian says. "Either financial or emotional. Most of us need one or the other or both."

Kara says, "When I'm broke, I think I should get married. Every time I can't buy something I want, I say, 'Damn, I'll just get married!' "

Jessica says the security she seeks is probably "emotional." She doesn't need a man to help support her children; their father supports them. She and I are both lucky in our custodial arrangements. Our children have the same economic life-style they had before divorce. For that reason, I have come to regard joint custody as the key ingredient in my successful divorce. I am not sure what I would have done if I had sole custody of Richard and not received enough child-support money to raise him in style. Would I have married the first man who asked, if I'd had to send my son off to school in hand-me-down clothes with his government-subsidized lunch ticket in his pocket? I would have at least considered it.

Carolyn, a WASP retail sales clerk in Lawrence, Kansas, says, "There are days when I would marry the first man with a decent income, the first guy who asked. I didn't get divorced so I could be alone; I got divorced because I had grand illusions about what marriage should be. I was a romantic; and my marriage wasn't romantic. So I left."

When Carolyn left four years ago, at age thirty, she regarded poverty as something of a grand adventure. "I knew it would be tight at first, but I told myself it would get better. I compared my new life to the beginning of my marriage, when we had been broke most of the time because Paul was finishing school.

"Well, I forgot one thing: Paul had a future when I married him. I didn't have a future when I married me."

When I met Carolyn last year on an assignment in Kansas, she was very realistic about money. A petite brunette who worried about the gray hairs coming in around her temples and the dimples in her thighs when she was married, Carolyn had become "a one-issue woman. The issue, political or personal, is money."

Her two children, Jessie, seven, and Jenny, nine, don't understand why they can't have all the toys they see advertised on television, why they can't stop at a fast food restaurant whenever they drive past one, why some kids have designer jeans and they don't.

"They just don't understand why things are so tight. I can't blame them. Jessie asked me last week, 'Why do you work, Mommy, when we can't have anything with your money?' Jenny still remembers living with her father and having mostly what she wanted. They both contrast our life-style to their dad and stepmother's. They think I am mean and stingy; I know they do."

When Carolyn left her marriage, she thought little about money. "It was just *there*. I spent all my time thinking about how I wanted a man who would talk to me. My husband worked all the time; and he isn't a garrulous, demonstrative man."

After she had been divorced a year, she woke up one morning worrying about money and realized she seldom thought about anything *but* money. "I cried. All the time I was married to Paul, I really hadn't worried about money, because it was his job. I'd never appreciated what a job it is until that morning; and I cried for not knowing what he went through for us all those years."

Now her life is circumscribed by stringent financial limitations: "My take-home pay is usually a little under $800 a month. The $250 child-support check I am supposed to be getting doesn't always arrive and never on time. You don't manage money under those circumstances. You manage the bills by deciding who can be put off for a few days, who won't wait, and who won't take your check to the bank before you've had a chance to cover it.

"I bounce checks. I never thought I'd reach the point in my life where I acted so poor and irresponsible. But sometimes my calculations don't work out. The check gets to the bank before I can cover it."

That happened to Carolyn several months ago when she wrote an "emergency" check for cash—cash that wasn't hers to claim because she had outstanding checks that would leave her balance at near zero when they came back to the bank. "Jenny had a sore throat and fever. I had to take her to the doctor and fill her prescription at the drug store. Well, that meant the telephone check bounced when it hit the bank a few days later. It wouldn't have if my support check had arrived on time.

"I called Paul the day I went to the doctor with Jenny and wrote the check to cover it. He promised he'd get the money to me right away. He didn't. The phone company called me at work a week later and said they were holding my check for $15.78 and would disconnect the phone the next day if they didn't have the money. My face was hot and red; and I wanted to bawl in front of my customers. Well, that day when I got home the check from Paul was in the mailbox. I had to scrape together change in the morning to get enough gas in the car to go cash Paul's check and recover my check at the phone company. Then I had to go to the grocery and make lunches for the kids and drop them off at school because we were also out of lunch food when they left in the morning.

"Fortunately, I was able to trade hours with another woman so I didn't have to lose work time to clear up this mess. But you can't believe how snippy they were to me at the phone company over a lousy $15.78. People who have no money have no power—and get no respect. I didn't realize these things when I was married and sheltered. When I was someone's wife with a steady income coming into my household, I was more a person than I am now. Living alone is a marginal existence. I don't know any men now, but if I did I would be looking for a husband and not for the idealistic reasons I thought I'd have when I divorced.

"When I hear a girl at work who's never been married talk about what she wants from a marriage, I think she's crazy. Then I laugh at myself: What she wants is exactly what I wanted when I left the marriage I had. I'm smarter now. What I want now is a decent living. If I find someone who isn't mean to me or my kids, who makes good money, I don't care if he talks to me or not. I want what I had."

Like many ex-wives, Carolyn resents the fact that Paul remarried, within a year, to a woman who also has a good job. "Between them, they make a lot of money. My kids sure don't see it. I blame her mostly for that; he is under her thumb. When I call to tell her about our problems—and I usually get her because he's at work or the health club—she tells me I should manage my money better. She says I shouldn't consider child-support money regular income. It's 'extra' money.

"I hate her. Worse than I hate him, I hate her."

Carolyn admits she hasn't pursued all the legal options now open to her in collecting child support. Government is now on the side of custodial mothers. Forcing men to pay is easier than it ever has been.

She also "makes it as difficult as possible" for Paul and his new wife to visit the children. She doesn't see the connection between regular visitation and regular support payments. Many lawyers, child psychologists, and other professionals believe there is one: Fathers who remain involved in their children's lives are far more likely to keep up regular support payments.

Carolyn says, "Maybe I am punishing him by withholding the kids. Isn't he punishing me by withholding money? If he paid on time and was more willing to help out with extra expenses, I would relent. He could change the visitation days when he has to be out of town; I would say yes when they call on the spur of the moment and ask to take the kids out for pizza. But why should I relent first?"

She doesn't think the solutions for her, or the kids, will be found in negotiating with her ex-husband.

"My kids need a father. I know they do. I want to find a husband for their sakes as much as mine. Next time, I'll be glad for what I have. And I'll finish my education in case I have to work again."

I've heard so many divorced mothers say they are looking for second husbands in part to "give the kids a father." This makes no sense to me. The kids already have a father. Isn't a real father preferable to a stepfather? Wouldn't Carolyn, and most divorced mothers, improve life by forging a closer tie between the children and the father they have? Are "fathers" interchangeable like so many little Fischer-Price play family people.

No, they aren't. But I can understand how Carolyn and her sisters have fallen into the trap of thinking they are.

Women who have so little real power in the world do have power as mothers. And we don't want to give it up—especially now that we've been out in the world a while and have had a chance to assess our power there. Maybe the single mom appeals to us as heroine because she has reduced the father's role to its lowest terms—inseminator—and proven women still rule somewhere. We can do it without them, but they can't do it without us.

For the most part, they seem to be willing to accept that.

Paternal custody, though increasing, is still rare, accounting for only 5 percent of custody decisions. Ted Kramer, the fictional hero of *Kramer vs. Kramer,* was a 1970s man. And joint custody, though more widely accepted now, is still opposed by many, including women's groups, which fear it will jeopardize women's financial stability by eliminating or reducing child support. (Statistics show otherwise: Joint-custody fathers, when they make more money than mothers, do pay child support and are more likely to pay it regularly than noncustodial fathers.)

But maternal custody is still the socially approved choice. And joint-custody mothers (or those who grant custody to fathers) are usually middle- or upper-middle-class women with careers—women who have some power other than maternal might.

Custody and support problems notwithstanding, the formerly married women with children I've interviewed seem to be happier than women who don't have children. Our kids do provide intimacy, solace, love. They are people to hug, with whom to share tears and laughter. Sometimes it's hard to share that love even with their fathers and new stepmothers.

Often the lives we are leading as single heads of a household struggling to keep it all together have led us to become dependent on those children for emotional support.

Carolyn says, "Because there's no man in my life, I often find myself telling Jenny my troubles. Maybe I tell her too much. When she goes to the grocery store with me she worries I won't have enough cash in my wallet to pay for everything. If Jessie puts something in the cart, she'll pull it out and ask me if it's okay, if we can afford it.

"I know I've done this to her by confiding too much, but what can you do? My kids and I are closer now than we ever were when I was married. All I have is my kids. I lost everything else in the divorce: our house, my charge accounts, most of my friends. I've only got the kids. Men get everything else.

"I never meant to end up this way."

I never meant to end up this way.

So few of us did. Women, who a decade ago were angry at men, at the institution of marriage, at the sexist society that fostered traditional marriage—are angry at themselves for not getting married when they had the proposals, for not staying married when they had husbands.

Carolyn is a very angry woman. She has plenty of reasons to be angry, legitimate targets for her anger: She is underpaid and exploited in her job. Her child-support checks, inadequate as they are, do not arrive on time. She has all the physical responsibility of parenthood. And she hasn't had a date in nearly a year, a sexual relationship in almost two years.

But she's angry at herself and at Paul's second wife—not at her employer, or Paul, or her parents, who told her she didn't need a college degree because she would get married, or at her lawyer, who doesn't do anything for her at all.

And nobody talks about housework anymore—much less gets irate about it. Jillian says, "We just accept the fact that women do most of it. We don't argue, do we?"

We have redirected our anger back at ourselves, where traditionally women have placed their anger: "It's my fault because . . ." Or we are angry at the women who have replaced us in our former homes, the women who have married our husbands and our lovers, the women who have found men while we have not.

We aren't angry at men as we were in the 1970s. They are no longer the problem. We want them to be the solution, if only they will. We want what our mothers wanted, only more.

We don't look at a failed marriage anymore and see the failure of marriage or of husbands. We see personal failures of wives with a small *w,* husbands with a small *h.* And each of us hopes she will be different, not like them.

Jessica, who was once "furious" at her husband, seldom gets "upset" at Eric. Oh, she would like him to "talk more." Then, he would like her to cook more meals.

"So we have compromised. Since cooking means so much to him, I cook meals if he will come in the kitchen and talk to me while I cook."

But Jessica hates to cook.

Did she mean to end up this way? She will only say that she is happy and in love.

Four conversations about marriage, all taking place within the last month, crystallized the "marriage issue" for me. Collectively, we have forgotten what we knew a decade ago about the interrelationships between money and dependence, happiness and self-respect. Maybe we want to forget.

Maggie, thirty, a successful Philadelphia banker: "I won't get married unless I find a very rich man.

"I can make a good living on my own; and there's no reason to marry unless I find a man who can give me more than I can give myself. I love to travel; and I don't want children. My work consumes most of my time. So why marry?

"If I do marry, I'll quit work. I'll do the things that interest me. Maybe I'll take up painting. I don't know if I'll have children or not. I just know I won't work. He has to be rich."

Paula, black, thirty, divorced mother of an eight-year-old son, teacher of handicapped children: "I want to get married because I'm tired of working.

"I want to take a year off; and I can't do that unless I have a husband. I wouldn't give up my independence. I'd still have a joint checking account and do whatever I wanted to do with the money in it. Marriage wouldn't change me. I wouldn't be dependent on a man just because he supported me."

Claire, fifty, WASP, copywriter, about to be unemployed: "I'll get married when I really need the security, like if I don't find another job now.

"I have a man who would marry me in a minute. He doesn't know about my married lovers. I keep everything from him so he'll still be there when I need him. He already has made me a beneficiary of his insurance policies."

Dana, thirty-eight, married, college English teacher: "Did the women's movement really happen? I can't believe the twenty-three- and twenty-four-year-old women in my department working on their master's degrees. They are so dependent on men. One of them checked herself into the hospital last week. She and her boyfriend had broken up. She can't cope.

"When I was separated [from her husband] six years ago, I threw myself into work, exercise, social activities. I made new friends. I never looked or felt so good. The end of a relationship should inspire women to make more of their own lives.

"What's wrong? Did the women's movement happen or didn't it?"

Or is that a question one can only ask from within the security of marriage?

8

Work: Where We Have Been

Self-actualization, usefulness, financial security and fun may only be as far away as your first paycheck.
— from *Getting Yours*
by Letty Cottin Pogrebin (1975)

. . . The world is beginning to accept the idea that a woman can make decisions in an office as well as cakes in a kitchen or seams in a garment factory—it is even beginning to realize that the fully productive woman is a vital asset to society.
—from *How to Go to Work When Your Husband Is Against It, Your Children Aren't Old Enough, and There's Nothing You Can Do Anyhow* (1972) by Felice N. Schwartz, Margaret H. Schifter, and Susan S. Gillotti

In the 1970s women discovered work. We dressed up our jobs and called them careers, then showed them off like babies in prams.

Work was supposed to be our means of fulfillment, our answer to the question "From what chief source will our lives derive meaning?" Every decade seems to have the answer for women: marriage and motherhood in the fifties, sex and politics in the sixties. Work was the new panacea, the promised land. You could, and should eventually, have everything else, but first you must have work. Surely no mass of people, male or female, ever romanticized work more than American women in the 1970s.

Magazines, including pace-setting *New York,* ran cover stories on two-career couples. We read them to learn how these young dynamos found time for each other and their household chores while amassing a fortune in Cuisinarts, microwaves, video recorders. It was the only way to be married.

The media focused heavily on working women: glamorous executives, trail-blazing scientists, doctors, engineers, women who had broken into blue-collar fields and were laying bricks, driving earth movers. They represented a minority of working women, yet they came to symbolize all of us. That image beckoned and enticed the American woman out of her home as the frilly-aproned happy housewife once lured her in.

Never married women graduated from college, bypassed marriage, and began working. They were the first group of women to put off marriage and motherhood for work. Aptly dubbed the "postponing generation," they were once again the cutting edge.

We married women envied them and the distaff halves of super-couples. They were "doing it right," whereas we had obviously done it all wrong, miring ourselves in diaper silt before our degrees were earned, our names inscribed in brass desk plates, or painted on law office doors. Our other question, part two of "What will give meaning to my life?" was "But can I work and be a good mother too?" We wanted to hear the answer, the unqualified yes, that the media gave us. We had to believe in quality time; it was our ticket out of the suburbs.

We went to work. And when our marriages fell apart, we worked harder.

As we had influenced sexual behavior and politics in the 1960s we changed the workplace in the 1970s. At the beginning of the decade, there were 31.6 million American women in the work force; by the end of the decade, we numbered 46.9 million. In the decade between 1972 and 1983, the number of women in professional, technical, and managerial positions increased by almost 41 percent.

To help each other get ahead, we formed network groups, those highly structured organizations created to counteract the loosely structured, underground unions of men, known as the old boys network. Men helped their buddies find jobs, land clients, close deals. They did business over lunch, on the golf course, at the clubs where we couldn't gain admittance. So we gathered in a quasi-social arena of our own, exchanged business cards, job leads, and the names of hot prospects over white wine and dinners, which were more often than not shaped and pressed beef patties and frozen peas, iceberg lettuce and tomato salads dripping Italian dressing. At first we were idealistic about networks. For some of us they replaced those consciousness raising groups we joined in the early 1970s that helped us get out of our marriages; and we expected intense emotional experiences here too. For others, they were an extension of study groups in the dorms and were expected to deliver the same results: helping the novice pass the exams.

We began to look at each other for business role models. For the first time, we weren't taking all our job cues from men. We knew *men* weren't thrilled to have us competing as equals on their playing fields. They liked us better as assistants, secretaries, helpers. We didn't trust the men on the job any more than we had trusted the men who were our husbands, our boyfriends.

We turned women in the workplace issues into political issues: We demanded equal pay for equal work and fought against sexual harassment on the job, unequal hiring and promoting practices, policies that discriminated against women. We bought John T. Molloy's book *Dress for Success* (1975) and followed his advice. We borrowed navy blue and gray suits from men, added silky ties, wore sensible shoes, and carried leather attaché cases. The object was no longer to marry the boss, as it had been for career girls before us. The object was to *become* the boss.

What we expected from our jobs was no less than what we had expected from sex, pot, politics: the ultimate high, a perfection of experience unmatched by anything our mothers had known.

I spent a lot of time in the 1970s writing about women in the workplace; and so I met many working women. I became familiar with each breed: the new young management women, executives full of confidence and high expectations; pink-collar workers in traditional women's jobs now devalued; blue-collar women, including pioneers who drove huge trucks or tarred roofs; older successful women in business and professions enjoying new respect as matriarchs. Most were seeking emotional, even spiritual, fulfillment on the job, but some few had no illusions about why they worked: They had to support themselves at something. That knowledge gave them a hard edge the newly crowned MBAs didn't have.

Pursuing business stories for *St. Louis* magazine or one of the

national trade publications for which I was a stringer, I rode in
many elevators going up at 8:00 A.M., mentally separating the secretaries from the management women by their clothes. I remember
reading—or maybe I wrote—this advice to secretaries: If you aspire
to management, carry a briefcase to work, even if it contains nothing
but your tuna sandwich. Image was all; and shouldn't everyone
aspire to management? Didn't we believe any woman who wanted
to get there could?

The message we gave secretaries was very similar to the one we
gave housewives: "Yes, dear, your work is necessary, *but* . . ." It
was delivered in the same haughty tone of voice. Or print.

Sometimes I interviewed secretaries. Many had college degrees
and aspirations and believed for a while that it was possible to move
from the typing pool to the executive suite. But mostly my subjects
were management women who complained the secretaries didn't
accept their authority. (And they were usually right. The secretaries
didn't.)

These management women who shared their secrets of success
were indeed young: under thirty, often only twenty-five, twenty-
six, twenty-seven. Young men in similar positions were not asked
for advice or opinions. Only their wives, lovers, and friends were
subject to their inanities. Invariably, the women told me how they
planned to run the company someday and marry and have children
between promotions. They would have it all; and they were sure
nothing would interrupt their climb to the top. Frequently they
sounded silly, but so would have their young male counterparts if
asked to pontificate on the corporate world or "how to mix work
with home and hearth."

One unforgettable new woman, a petite blonde, told me she had
worked out all the details for her pregnancy, which would take
place in exactly five years, one year after her thirtieth birthday and
her wedding to the perfect man she had yet to meet. She would
work until she went into labor, stay home for three weeks, four
maximum, during her company's slow season, breast-feed baby via
a breast pump, which she would use to collect her milk while on
the job.

"But what if something goes wrong?" I asked her. "If you have
a difficult pregnancy or birth—or if the baby is born with health
problems?"

"Oh," she said, "nothing will go wrong."

I never thought to ask, as I would ask now, "But what if you can't find a husband or can't get pregnant when you're ready?"

Everywhere I went I asked women about their aspirations, their experiences. The answers often made me wonder if they were following yet a new emperor wearing a different new set of clothes. They were still striving to become the embodiment of a media myth. She was no longer the happy housewife; she was Superwoman instead.

I met Sheron in November 1976. I remember the month and year because the charter issue of *Working Woman* magazine had just been published; and we both pulled out our copies almost simultaneously. We were sitting side by side on a plane bound for Chicago, where she still lives.

Now thirty-six, Sheron is black, a strikingly beautiful corporate executive at one of the Fortune 500 companies. She calls herself a "bumpie," a black upwardly mobile urban professional. Ten years ago she says she was a "scared kid with an MBA and no idea that she was the hottest marketing concept of the decade: an educated black woman." She thought she would have a hard time finding a job; instead she had a hard time deciding which job offer to accept.

When I met her, she'd already been working a year. There were no traces of the "scared kid" in her public persona. I thought she was the epitome of the New Woman. *I* was the scared kid, newly divorced, flying out of St. Louis on my first business trip. I was relieved to be sitting beside her so I could watch her and see how she behaved.

"When I got out of college, I knew I didn't want to be married when there was so much happening for women. I broke an engagement with my college sweetheart and rented a studio apartment. It was the first time I had ever lived alone. I was so eager last year. All I really wanted was the chance to prove I could do a good job.

"After I got my first paycheck, I realized I also cared about having things. I saw that white women, especially pretty ones, can get things through men. Not many black women, even pretty ones, can. I was determined to get things for myself.

"Well, I've been lucky. I got out of school at the height of affirmative action. Everybody wanted to hire and promote blacks and women. With me, they got two for one.

"After I'd been in my job for two months, *only two months,* my first boss told me how relieved he was that I could 'think.' 'What do you mean?' I asked him. 'Could someone incapable of thinking get this job?' He was surprised I didn't understand that I was hired *because* I was a black woman, not in spite of it. And he was just glad the obligatory black woman was not a dunce."

Nine years later, Sheron describes this conversation as her "baptism of disillusionment. I'm glad it happened early. Some of my friends, especially white women, went for years before they found out what the real operating rules were. When they finally did, they were terribly disappointed. But until they did, there was a barrier between us. I knew something they didn't or had still refused to learn."

Though disillusioned, Sheron never considered not "playing the game."

The only alternative, she says, "was to cop out or marry out. In the 1970s, no one with an MBA was marrying out and few were copping out. I knew two women MBAs who threw over business for social work or the arts. The rest of us stayed. The lure of money, power, was too strong."

Sheron, an only child, was the first college graduate in her family, the first to hold a white-collar job—fulfilling her parents' dreams for her. "All my cousins got pregnant, then married, most before they finished high school." Her (late) father was a laborer; her mother still works as a licensed practical nurse at a Chicago hospital.

"She loves her work," Sheron says, "because she loves looking after people. Sometimes she gripes about the shit she takes from nurses or doctors, but it's good-natured griping. I never could complain in that resigned fashion she has mastered.

"Even in the early days, when I got together with other women executives for a bitch session, it was a real bitch session. Somebody was always saying, 'Well, what are we going to do about this?' or 'How do we circumvent this jerk's authority?'

"My mother has never thought about changing things in her workplace. We took it as a given that we would make some changes. But, looking back, I think our vision was not sweeping enough. We were too anxious to learn their game rules, wear their playing outfits, fit into their man-made system. We didn't want enough change; we didn't ask enough from them. We just wanted our share; and we were willing to work more than our share to get it."

Sheron fell into the ten- or twelve-hour workday habit early in her first job. She took home a briefcase laden with reading material every weekend. As soon as she had her own key to the office building, she made "regular pilgrimages to the altar of my desk on Sundays.

"Partly, coming in on Sunday was form. You did certain things to get ahead. It was good to be seen by the upper echelon; and the place was empty enough on Sunday to be seen. You put in hours rather than worked efficiently so you'd appear dedicated. It was better to be seen in the office than to work at home.

"Partly, it was genuine obsession. I was alive at work in a way I wasn't alive anywhere else. Even when I got disillusioned, when I realized I wasn't going to change corporate America, but it was going to change me—I was caught up in the whole thing. Like a heroin addict.

"And I've always liked coming in on Sundays because it filled the day. Sleep late, read the papers, drive to the office. I've never had an office I didn't love."

Sheron belonged to three network groups during the 1970s. She was a founding mother of the first group, which was nonexclusive in terms of membership criteria and not aligned with any one profession. Most of the members also belonged to professional groups within their own professions.

"We thought it was important to accept any woman who wanted to belong. Part of our avowed philosophy was to help entry-level women make it up the ladder, to encourage secretaries to move into management. We had dinner meetings with programs and speakers. The speakers talked to us about investing our money, controlling our body language, learning to use home computers, dressing for success.

"During the social hours before and after meetings women exchanged business cards. Theoretically, if you were looking for a new position or you needed to hire an accountant, you could meet your needs within the group. Sometimes it worked. I did find my tax accountant in the group. In the 1970s we were all members for a while. Nobody ever skipped a meeting for a date with a man—or admitted to doing that at least.

"I really got involved initially because I wanted to help other black women. There weren't many to help.

"That first year of networking was a euphoric time. Well, maybe it was more like six months of euphoria. Then we divided into groups within groups. We spent a lot of time deciding on rules of order and how much to charge for dues. The women who were far ahead in careers carried the weight. Some of them resented it. One of them told me she felt like prom queen because she was always being courted. Women were after her the way men once were, for what she symbolized, not who she was.

"But to be fair, some of the older successful women liked being in this position. They were finally getting the approval of their sex, something denied them by snotty car-pool mothers."

Sheron stayed with this group for three years, because she felt "it was the thing to do. I was job hopping a lot, moving from one company to another, and up very fast. I never knew who I would need next year that I might have met at some meeting. So I stayed in the group and circulated like mad. The last two years it was just something I did."

In those early days management women may have had husbands, but they didn't have babies—or talk about them if they did. One certainly didn't rush home from such a gathering to relieve the sitter. Sheron remembers the night when a young woman brought her baby to a meeting.

"She apologized profusely for bringing him. The sitter hadn't shown up; and she had wanted badly to hear the speaker. She promised to leave if he whimpered.

"He couldn't have been more than a few months old and slept through most of the evening. He didn't fuss. You wouldn't believe the angry stares she got. One woman complained loudly that the umbrella stroller created a safety hazard. It certainly didn't. I felt sorry for the baby's mother."

By 1979, Sheron was a junior vice-president with a small firm. Her picture was in *Chicago* magazine. She was featured in the *Chicago Tribune*'s business section. "I was black, smart, successful, young. I was riding high. It was a trip, a trip I couldn't have taken in any other era. The 1970s really were the women's decade if you fit the ideal and worked hard and of course got there first.

"It was worth the price."

After reaching VP status, Sheron dreaded network meetings because "I was such a visible success symbol, people were after me for something the minute I walked in the door. At first I fell into that trap of promising to do too much, things I probably couldn't do—and then not delivering on my promise.

"Women do that a lot because we want to be good and liked. It's hard to say no. But I learned the hard way it's easier than saying yes and not following through."

When she was asked to join an exclusive group of women, all at the VP level or its equivalent for their profession, she accepted.

"I had some qualms about it. There weren't supposed to be queen bees anymore; and here we were setting ourselves up in a gilded hive. In a way it was selling out the women below. But really they didn't have anything to contribute to our group."

Sheron says, "We tried to dignify and justify ourselves by setting up task forces to investigate workplace issues. I was on one to deal with sexual harassment.

"In the late 1970s it was dangerous even to flirt at work. Those were uptight times. Everyone was investigating harassment. We were taking ourselves very seriously. It got crazy for a while. We listened to a complaint from a woman who told us a man laid his hand on her arm. On the other hand, the really blatant stuff still went on behind closed doors.

"But I do think we did some good. We accomplished something. If you asked me what's the most important thing women did for other women in the late 1970s, I would say it was to force sexual harassment out of the closet, make it an issue, label it a corporate crime. Maybe we didn't stop it all, but we made everyone admit it exists. Women who had been afraid to speak up had support. Even if they were still afraid, they knew for the first time harassment wasn't their fault.

"It had been like rape: something women blamed on themselves. *I must have led him on.* We made people see harassment is a power play, not an act of lust. We changed the whole perception."

The development of networks and the fight against harassment are to the 1970s and women what the antiwar movement was to the 1960s and students.

But Sheron says, "The networks were not nearly so successful. They may have been sisterhood's last blast. Networking by group works if you're smart enough not to expect too much from a group and clever enough to know how to get as much as you can—but then if you're that smart, that opportunistic, you really have corrupted the original intent, haven't you?

"On the other hand, if you go into it like sister angel and try to be everybody's friend, you're not living and dealing in the real world, are you?"

The crux of the networking dilemma.

It was tempting to see the groups as clusters of friends or potential friends. After centuries of practice, men were able to separate the friendly business associate from the friend; but we had had no practice. Too many of us went out there and tried to make friends out of every woman in a navy skirted suit. And inevitably we were disappointed.

My own networking experiences were disappointing. I helped form a group of women writers in the fall of 1978. We had no professional criteria for membership. And we secretly believed undiscovered women of great talent in the St. Louis area were waiting for our hand-lettered announcement to appear on bulletin boards in women's centers and bookstores so they could blossom under our tutelage.

We attracted a grandmother who had published a letter in the country journal; several neurotic young women who wrote bad poetry about wicked mothers, fathers, stepmothers, husbands; a woman who wrote short stories starring a blond princess who was really she—and a lot of women who wanted to use my name as an entrée at the city magazine. Serious writers, especially paid professionals, attended one meeting, mumbled excuses about deadlines or sick cats at home vomiting on the carpet, and left early. They looked elsewhere for their network fix. (Lynne went to one meeting and labeled us the Feminiques.)

We had our first group crisis over a man. He belonged to one of the poets. I flirted with him; and she sent the group a long letter resigning.

Midway through our short year of existence some of us realized we should have established criteria for membership, but it was too late. Our treasurer was not published. Besides, we still hadn't decided who, as a group, we were. How could women who gathered in a sitting room swathed in afghans and patchwork quilts, sipping from teacups and wine glasses set down among the wilted plants and a sleeping kitten—how could such cozy women eliminate anyone?

During the year, I also attended meetings of another network group, a larger, more structured organization open to any woman in business or the professions. It had taken them six months to write a constitution, but they seemed to have their act together when it was finished. They also seemed to have the same problems our little group had: A few women dominated the group; the constant flow of new faces necessitated unduly long periods of introduction each time; some women needed too much, gave too little.

Too many women still had too little to share—except work stories. Everyone had a chauvinist-boss tale. Each could remember being harassed, underpaid, unfairly bypassed for promotion—all the Click! stories of the workplace; and we told them endlessly to each other. They were our equivalent of the male war stories; but we told them with white wine, not beer, in our hands.

In our little group the stories were just as likely to be personal, about mothers, husbands who kept us down, who didn't want us to write—and thus provided subject matter for most of what we did write, the odes to breaking free. (And then when winter came, most of the poets were afraid to drive on ice.)

Women frequently called me in those days asking for guidance in finding the perfect group. Like the princess sleeping on a pile of feather beds, we felt the hard pea beneath. We were uncomfortable, restless, in each group. We talked about finding groups that suited our needs when we joined, yet continued to grow apace with us. Do you see the similarity in network groups and perfect marriages/relationships with men? Well, the groups didn't exist either.

The large organizations seemed impersonal to me. But our little group of women was too personal. And ineffective. Though one of our initial goals had been to help everyone publish, at the end of the year none of the unpublished writers had published. We read works aloud, ostensibly to critique them, so they could be honed to perfection, then sold—but nobody ever said anything negative in the critiques that followed the readings. We were more encounter group than professional organization, but we failed as an encounter group too. We praised, encouraged, *lied*. The truth might have saved us.

I was very frustrated with those women who didn't want to make money at their writing. Women in the larger network were frustrated with other women who didn't exhibit suitably aggressive tendencies about getting ahead. For a sisterhood, we were remarkably intolerant of each other and growing more so as the decade played out.

A journalist who attended our writers guild meetings once or twice told me, "I think your group failed because you tried to be all things to all women." We, the "core group" of four, did try to mother the distraught women working out their therapy on paper, mentor the fledglings, befriend each other. Our failures eventually made us resentful of them, of each other.

We only got it together once. And I remember that night as my personal bright shining moment in the decade of women: We met at the home of Patti, a lesbian, and her lover, Denise. They had cleaned and polished and cooked; and the old house they were renovating glowed with their physical efforts and general good spirits. We were as we had been in those first few meetings: accepting of each other, eager to know how our sisters felt and thought. The little lines of disapproval we had begun to wear in each other's presence were smoothed over for this night.

We had our only guest speaker, a man who had written his Ph.D. dissertation on Flannery O'Connor. His wife accompanied him at our invitation; in lieu of a fee, he let us take up a collection for the sitter. When he talked about Flannery O'Connor, gender distinctions faded away. Like a literary clairvoyant conducting a seance, he brought her to life in that room. And we didn't get the feeling that he appreciated "women's writing." She was a writer to him, not a woman writer.

This is what I think women had been striving for: a gathering of people indifferent to race, creed, gender, and sexual preference who shared their work, who talked passionately about ideas that were important to them. And we made it for one night.

And at the end of a year we split for very personal reasons; some of us were prochoice and some were antiabortion; the straights felt uncomfortable hearing descriptive poems about lesbian sex. Those of us who worked for a living were disdainful of those who wrote little poems and lived like mice in holes provided by mothers, boyfriends, ex-husbands. We had been so proud of ourselves for our diversity. At the end, we didn't like the person the other was; we wanted her to be more like us. It was late 1979; and much of the romance was gone from work, from networking, from revolutions of all kinds.

I spent an hour with Sheron at O'Hare Airport in Chicago waiting for a plane in December 1979. Of course we speculated on what the 1980s might bring for women. She was almost thirty; and she said the younger women made her feel old.

"Younger women always do that." I told her about Elizabeth, a public relations writer who called me sometimes for advice. Her clear sweet voice and the sound of her baby gurgling in the background always made me feel like old Susan, patroness of the press release.

"This is different," Sheron said. "It's a different way of feeling old, like I went to Vietnam and came back and discovered nobody knew there'd been a war.

"These women think equal pay exists. They actually debate whether ERA is necessary. You know I didn't think of myself as a feminist until this new group came along and said they didn't want the label. I wanted to tell them, 'You wouldn't be anywhere without Friedan and Steinem.' They expect so much. Well, so did we, but we have always carried in the back of our minds at least a sense of the price we would pay for it. And they don't. They don't believe in paying. They don't think they have to put off anything.

"A lot of the women I know have gotten married or engaged this year. I think some of them settled. And I think we knew all along we would have to settle someplace.

"At least I did."

I think she was the exception.

9

Work: Where We Are Now

*The newest trend in office romance is not between woman
and coworker, but between woman and work. The hot
question still remains: Will she get burned?*
—from *Working Woman*, November 1984

D on't women always get burned in romance? Why should this
time be different?

Work has become, either by design or chance, the replacement for love in many of our lives. The catchphrase for women
who marry their jobs is "corporate nun." Some of these "nuns" are
celibate for long stretches of time—either because their limited social lives don't expose them to available men or the men they meet
are so far beneath their standards, they prefer chastity. They've
married the corporation, not a man, not a church.

Did they really expect work to be a better bridegroom than husbands were?

The *Good Housekeeping* for the corporate bride, *Working Woman*,
may not have faced this yet, but the honeymoon is over. In this
marriage, however, divorce may not be a possibility. Women cannot
afford to exit the workplace as they entered it: en masse.

As of October 1984 (according to statistics provided by the *New
York Times*) 50 million women were at work. More than two-thirds
of women aged twenty-five to fifty-four, married and single, held
jobs. And three out of five mothers of dependent children were
working outside the home. We can't afford a divorce. Yet some of
us are beginning to want, if not divorce from our jobs, then periodic
separations.

Part of our career angst we share with men. We are all coming
to terms with the elemental truth of the baby-boom generation:

Most of us won't achieve all our goals. Our expectations have been too high, and our numbers too great for all those expectations to be met. Yes, we are all a little disappointed. Men and women alike have begun to look outside the workplace for personal satisfaction, but men, more easily than we, can find a partner to assuage their little griefs.

And the bloom is off the MBA, the degree that was supposed to give us total happiness, just as the title "Ms." was supposed to do once upon a time. The MBA is no longer a fast-track ticket to success. Now the experts tell us: If it's not the *right* MBA from the *right* school, it won't even get us hired by the *right* company.

A decade ago we were also told not to let our children keep us down. Put them in day care. Well, affordable day care is almost impossible to find. Scandals about sexual and physical abuse and neglect of children in centers have been covered in frightening detail by the press. New studies warn us that our kids are far more likely to contract various diseases if they spend time in day-care centers. The guilt of the working parent has increased. Only a very well-employed single mother can afford to be totally free of that guilt.

Obviously we have problems connected with working that men have never had to face. And we have been in the marketplace for a comparatively short period of time. Some of us are frustrated because we have reached our first plateaus. Others have found the secretarial jobs that were supposed to serve as stepping stones into management training only led to advanced word processing. And some of us are simply *tired* of working. No generation of women before us worked all their lives. We thought working was something women could choose, or choose *not*, to do.

Only a decade ago we still occupied the privileged, spoiled position of special people who didn't have to hold jobs. Even when we began working en masse, we didn't face the realities of the workplace. We believed we were entitled to *interesting, fulfilling* work. This belief may be in some part responsible for the continuing job disparity between men and women.

A gender pay gap still exists: The Bureau of Labor statistics for late 1984 quoted the average weekly earnings for men at $393, and for women at $260. The average male high school graduate still earns approximately the same as the average female college graduate. The disparity between males and females with postgraduate degrees in the forty-five-to-fifty-four age range is *more* than two to one.

Although women have made significant inroads into previously male-dominated occupations, our jobs are still concentrated in the low-paying occupations, such as clerical work, waitressing, retail sales, or low-paying industries such as textiles, shoes, and clothing manufacture. *Working Woman*'s 1985 salary report (published in the January issue) disclosed that in every field, even nursing, where 96 percent of the jobs are held by women, *men* outearn us.

Maybe they outearn us in part because they believe they are entitled to the best pay they can get—regardless of whether the work is "interesting" or "fulfilling." And they learned long ago what we have only recently discovered: Most jobs are not interesting, fulfilling, and fun. Even the jobs that seemed like they would be—or were for a while—have turned into that which must be done from Monday morning through Friday afternoon, fifty weeks a year. My God, it's never ending!

We don't want to retreat permanently behind the picket fences, but we would like a respite, a break now and again from the routine. Recent studies indicate 72 percent of the country's working women have dropped out of the work force for six months or more. The figures for professional women alone are surprising: They have spent an average of 23 percent of potential work years away from the work force, compared with 2 percent for men.

It can be argued, and justifiably so, that women are still the parents who stay home with babies—but professional women haven't had *that* many babies. Many married women take time out to pursue advanced degrees, train for another job, write a novel, learn a foreign language. Men, on the other hand, are expected to do those things after work.

As women, we still have a sense of entitlement; it is the noblesse oblige of the married woman. Single women can't stop working; and we envy those who can.

Over and over again, women tell me, "I am tired." Tired of working at low-paying jobs, of carrying the financial responsibility for a household alone, tired of living on one paycheck in a two-paycheck world. "I didn't think it would be like this," is how many women describe their work lives ten years later. The biggest economic trend of our times is the two-career marriage; and we are left out of it.

We look around and see married, pregnant businesswoman everywhere. Never married women fantasize about having their own babies, their own extended maternity leaves. Formerly married women fantasize about taking the kids out of day care for just one year.

Nothing has turned out exactly the way we thought it would. Work hasn't been the perfect husband either.

"Women could be happier married to their work, if work paid better," says Alicia. "A rich husband is *always* better."

In late December 1980, I went to see the movie *9 to 5* with Alicia, a very large, very unhappy blonde who had recently moved to Edwardsville from California. She and her son were staying with relatives while she, at thirty-three, tried to sort out her life and find work in St. Louis. "I'm not going to be a secretary anymore," she said. "It's a dead end. It's a pit." And *9 to 5* made her furious.

The hit comedy, starring Dolly Parton, Jane Fonda, and Lily Tomlin as secretaries who fight job inequities by kidnapping the boss, "didn't provide any real solutions to the problems of secretaries," Alicia said. "I expected better from Jane Fonda. She took the threat of nuclear energy plants seriously in *China Syndrome*. She's been serious about everything from the Vietnam War to her body—everything but secretaries. When she made a movie about us, she switched to comedy."

I liked *9 to 5*. So did a lot of secretaries. Others agreed with Alicia. I am not sure that moviegoers would have patronized a movie presenting a serious view of the secretarial dilemma. At least these three heroines were bold and aggressive women who joined forces against a chauvinist male.

The idea of working women joining together was touted by *Ms.* in January 1981 as "the new strength of women office workers in the 1980s." The nation's 20 million office workers were supposed to be organizing to make the workplace a more humane place. Women who work in the real world say it hasn't happened—and nobody talks about making it happen much anymore.

Alicia was determined not to be a secretary in 1980; and she finally took a position as an "administrative assistant with promotion potential." She hoped *this* job might be different than the others because *this* company might be looking at the secretary in a new, more positive light. She might really have a chance to move up. Alicia soon learned, not much to her surprise, only the name of the job was different; and the salary, $17,000 a year, was better than the salary she might have earned as a degreed woman employed in some other fields.

When she decided to accept that job, I took her out for a celebration drink. She wasn't feeling ebullient. "I know I'm coming to terms," she said. "But I don't have a choice. I have to stop messing up my life, moving in with men and out again and having no place for me and Jason to stay. I did that too much in California. I kidded myself too much there. I couldn't afford to live alone so I said I was in love. I was always going to be a writer, so I went to parties and called myself a screenwriter.

"I came out here because I had nowhere else to go. But it also feels good to be somewhere where I don't have to say I'm a screenwriter anymore. I have to come to terms with what I am, don't I?"

Even as she asked that question, she wasn't ready to call herself a secretary.

Six months later she found another man and moved to Boston with him, leaving Jason behind with her brother to finish the school year. ("If this were a real job, I wouldn't just pick up and go. But it isn't.") Then Jason's father came back into his life and Jason decided to live with him. Meanwhile, Alicia got a job in Boston. This time the job description labeled her a secretary and paid her $19,000. And the boss patted her on the ass.

She wrote, "I'm too tired to complain now. It really doesn't bother me anymore. If all he wants is an occasional pat, I can live with it. I make long-distance calls on the office phone to Jason; and I know my boss knows. So we're even."

On her 1984 Christmas card she wrote from Cleveland, where she was living with another man and working again as a secretary, "I have come to terms with my life. This time, I have. I may marry this man. Well, I will if he asks me. What I should have done was get a real career early; and I didn't. That's why it went this way, but it's okay now, really it is."

Alicia believes a career would have changed her life; and maybe it would have. And we thought 9 to 5 improved the image of the secretary, the average working woman. Suddenly we all saw her as a bright, witty, inventive woman coping imaginatively with paperwork overload, lack of respect, sexual harassment, office technology. Still, we hadn't begun to admit there were many more secretaries than management women—that there were in fact many more women holding all manner of low-salary, low-opportunity jobs than women who fit our new glamor model of working woman: she who resides in the executive suite.

How many formerly married women like Alicia had left the suburbs to find themselves inside this myth—and found the cold, impersonal workplace instead?

Even as the myth crumbled around them, they still glamorized career and blamed themselves for having only jobs. (Had their mothers or older sisters likewise blamed themselves for not being happy housewives rather than examine the myth, blame the culture that promoted it?) These women think they are failures. And "just a secretary (or sales clerk or nurse's aide)" has replaced "just a housewife" as the self-deprecating tag too many women use.

"I am a failure," Alicia says. And success is the American obsession. A large chunk of the books in our bookstores tell us how to succeed, to win at something, from losing weight to moving up. Women's magazines have made a cult of self-improvement. It is more difficult to qualify for new and improved all the time. Once a woman could be successful if she had shiny floors and made flaky pie crusts. Now she must have a career to be successful, to be happy.

We still believe success can make us happy. Ironically, women seem to believe this more now than men do. When the American Management Association polled managers in 1984, 60 percent of the women reported getting the greatest satisfaction in life from their careers, whereas only 37 percent of the men did. A male friend assured me, "We learned something from the women's revolution that you didn't learn. You told us to pay more attention to relationships, to stop making work the center of our lives. And we listened."

I reminded him he still has the numbers on his side: thousands of terrific women from which to choose. We have a handful of men who aren't married, gay, or nerds. No wonder we focus on work.

We willingly sacrificed personal relationships to success in the 1970s. How many women are still making the sacrifice today—and how many others really have nothing to sacrifice? How many of us continue to measure success strictly by our job titles because we have no other measure?

Sheron says, "In the 1970s corporate women played right into the hands of the male hierarchy; and now we are stuck with what we agreed upon.

"Just when a sizable portion of men were coming along who

questioned the necessity of transferring to new cities at corporate whim, who refused to put in one-hundred-hour weeks, who insisted on a life away from the office—we also came along. We didn't question any of that. Like good little girls, we did as they expected us to do.

"We accepted the rules. Yes, we were naive. But would we have been accepted any other way? Could we, as young women, have come in, like some young men did, and written our own rules? I don't think so."

Sheron is almost the 1980s version of Marie, the Belleville book-keeper mentioned earlier who made her job with a small family firm the core of her life. Sheron has more power, money, self-esteem. She's certainly less self-effacing and expects more recognition, more perks, more rewards from her work. But she has made work the focus of her life, excluding marriage and motherhood, because, like Marie, she honestly didn't think women could manage both worlds equally well.

"I hear about liberated marriages. What I have seen is not quite liberated. Several years ago, one of my friends and her husband were interviewed for a magazine story about the two-career mar-riage. They spouted all this stuff about shared chores and mutual respect for the other's work. Oh, he admitted cutely, she probably did 'a little more.' Reading the article one got the impression they were very close to equal. Not true.

"*She* takes time off from her job to check out day-care centers, take kids to doctors, attend parent conferences. *She* worries about organizing meals and assigning chores. *He* never does anything he isn't told or asked to do—anything she hasn't outlined for him. Is that equal?

"And the really insidious thing is they both think his work is a little more important than hers, though she makes more money, has the greater talent—and had the greater potential.

"I'm sure she'd be at the top of her profession someday without him and the two kids. With them, no, she won't be. She hasn't got the freedom to do it.

"Being at the top is more important to me than anything else. I do think I would have made different choices if I had known for some reason I wouldn't get this far. Then I might have taken time for a child, might have compromised and married one of the men I knew.

"Yes, I know: Some women thought they were going to get farther than they have or will—and now regret making this choice rather than the other one. They regret not going for marriage. They look at married women as mothers and think, 'They have it all, but I don't.'

"We always hear that successful men who have families have it all, but we never experience their lives firsthand to see if this is true, do we? I don't believe many male corporate dynamos have great marriages, close ties with their kids. They may have families that give them some pleasure—or maybe no pleasure at all—but do they really have it all? I doubt it."

Sheron does not feel the ambivalence about work many women report. The difference, she says, is "my money and job status. I have these things so I am happy. I could never quit working, even if I married a rich man. I'm work obsessed."

After she left her husband, Jessica was work obsessed for two years. Her struggle for perfection on the job replaced her quest to be the perfect wife and mother.

She says, "When my marriage ended, I took a new job with a brand new company. The president, Allen, and I were the only people here for the first few months. He really needed me to get the business off the ground; and I needed an outlet for my energy, my enthusiasm.

"So I put everything into working. I easily spent sixty or seventy hours at the office or out seeing prospective clients. Sometimes I came into work in the middle of the night, worked all day, and stayed past five again.

"One night I was ready to come to work at two, but it seemed too early. I drove down to the riverfront and watched the moon on the Mississippi for an hour or so until I felt it was okay to go into the office.

"I can get by on little sleep, a nap for an hour or so on the floor if I have to. Or if I go home at six, shower and catnap on the couch for an hour, I'm fine.

"And the work was really exciting, challenging. I got our first national client. We had a small regional piece of this client's business. I knocked myself out servicing the account, so we got a chance to make a presentation for the whole thing. And we got it. That was due largely to me."

The agency turned a profit from the start, but the national account marked a turning point, the beginning of an upsurge in business. The staff was expanded. And Allen, in appreciation for Jessica's work on landing the lucrative account, gave her the first promotion, a promotion that carried a raise of less than $100 a month. She was made a supervisor of other account executives shortly after she met Eric. A few days later she won a European vacation for two in a travel agency contest.

"I was high that week. It was my birthday. I got promoted. I was falling in love. I won a free trip; and I had a wonderful man to take along. I thought the kids were okay. It was probably the high point of my life when everything came together.

"Shortly after that, Dawn moved in with me. And the problems with her anorexia began again."

Jessica's own problems, as a supervisor, began almost immediately too.

Colleen recalls the announcement of Jessica's promotion at a Monday morning staff meeting: "It was met with disbelief, envy, and some unhappiness. Nobody thought it was a good idea. She was promoted past a senior account executive with several years of experience. She was put in charge of a woman who didn't trust her. And Allen, oblivious to all of these undercurrents of feeling, hadn't prepared anyone in advance."

Within a week, Jessica had clashed with Anne, an independent, highly competent account executive who admittedly "doesn't like working for women."

Jessica's supervisory style is close and critical. She writes voluminous notes in work critiques. Once she asked that a basic press release be rewritten twenty-three times. A perfectionist who, until Eric came into her life, spent most of it at the office, she is now handing much of her routine work to subordinates and demanding they perform it exactly as she would have done.

Recently Anne quit. Colleen has told Allen she won't work under Jessica. And Randy, another account executive assigned to Jessica, simply bypasses her authority most of the time.

He took the twenty-three copies of his press release into Allen's office and said, "You pick the best one." When Allen picked the second draft, Randy all but withdrew himself from Jessica's supervision.

Jessica excuses his defection by saying, "He'll come around." But

Anne's resignation angered and hurt her. "She just refused to work with me. I remember the first day I thought I was being effective as a supervisor. I went home that night and told Eric I felt really good about what I had accomplished. Well, Anne was in Allen's office about the same time complaining about me and threatening to quit. He begged her to stay; and she did for three more months. I wish he'd let her go then. I think she proves the evils of promoting from within. She was hired as a secretary; and she never should have been brought into account work."

Anne and Jessica played out their conflict by assuming very familiar adversarial positions. I've heard versions of this story told on the network circuit and from supervisors and managers in interviews for trade publications. Anne and Jessica took their complaints about each other to Allen, who did little more than relay what one had said to the other. The two women seldom dealt directly with each other and their mutual problems. Allen didn't deal with them effectively either. The entire staff became involved to some degree in the personality clash between the two women.

It reminds me of the disputes between women in the Catholic Parents' Club. They were taken to the priest; and he didn't handle them very well either.

Anne says, "I don't like working for more than one person at a time. Allen knew that from the start. When I started with him, I was a receptionist and secretary, responsible only to him. He quickly promoted me to special events coordinator, then account executive, always under his tutelage. I was used to working with him. And I felt like he broke a promise to me when he put Jessica in charge of me. She is not a good supervisor.

"I don't understand what made Allen put her in that position. There's been talk they were having an affair or at least had a strong attraction to each other. It is hard to understand otherwise, isn't it?"

Jessica retorts, "Well, Anne can afford to quit, can't she? Her husband has a good job. They don't need the money. She can take her time finding another position. She's quit other jobs. Isn't that her pattern?"

Colleen tried unsuccessfully to play peacemaker, which nearly cost her Jessica's friendship. She blames Allen: "He had no experience at managing people before he started the agency. Then he put Jessica in a supervisory position when she had no supervisory background. They both need management training.

"They are very loyal to each other; and I don't think that has anything to do with sex. You have to remember, they started the office together; and she was responsible for their biggest break. Unfortunately, their loyalty makes them blind to each other's faults. She was given a shockingly low raise for her new job, but she doesn't complain. She is largely responsible for the loss of camaraderie in the office, but he hasn't said anything to her about it. Besides, he isn't the type to admit he's made a mistake, which he did in promoting her.

"Losing Anne hurt a lot. She was good, the best account exec here in some areas. And it didn't need to happen. She was at the point in her life, age forty, where she wasn't going to put up with anything. Can you blame her? Would a man her age?"

The clash with Anne has taken some of the joy out of work for Jessica; once again she is disillusioned with a less than perfect groom. She also has her daughter's serious problems to face. Over the Christmas holidays Dawn threatened suicide, which automatically extended the length of her hospital stay.

"She's only okay," Jessica says. "Not good. I think it's going to take a very long time. She still has a lot of unresolved anger about the divorce. And she isn't willing to accept Eric and me."

The crisis has drawn Jessica and Eric closer together. She leaves work every day by 5:30 so she will be at his apartment at 6:00 when he arrives. She spends her nights in his bed, not her desk chair. And she doesn't leave his home in the morning until he does, in time for normal working hours.

"I'm still working hard. Work is still important to me. I was using it to fill up my life for a while, as an antidote to loneliness; and I don't have to do that anymore."

Clearly Jessica isn't in love with her job the way she once was. If the agency loses the juicy account, as both Allen and Jessica fear they will, the romance will probably cool further. Maybe Allen will be less impressed with her.

What's happening to Jessica sounds terribly personal. And these sound like the reflections on the possible fates of soap opera characters. But women personalize their jobs. Workplace conflicts are like the soaps.

Sheron says, "Women haven't been adequately prepared for many of the workplace responsibilities they've been given. They haven't had time to learn the personal detachment you need to manage people effectively. And the men who should have taught them, haven't. Women-to-women problems have surfaced all across the board in the last several years. Women still don't like working for each other. They often do use the available man as a buffer between themselves. Or they vie for his attention and favor. I don't put this kind of behavior down to biology. It's social conditioning of course. But it's a real part of the work force.

"An MBA does not prepare anyone for the realities outside business school. And the smaller the company, the more creative the field, the more you see women given responsibility without training, often because they will take on a lot more work for not much more money.

"There are shelves of books out there, including some very good ones, on how to deal with these problems. Unfortunately, they are not mandatory reading for working women."

Men may have had just as many supervisory and managerial problems as women. But Sheron thinks they are better prepared to deal with those problems "if for no other reason than they weren't told to expect bliss with the job.

"Women are getting massive doses of realism in the 1980s. When we first went to work, we were girl wonders. The girl, or boy, wonder stage only lasts so long. Eventually something has to go wrong. A job is like a car. You get the bugs out when it's new; and you think it's perfect. In six months or a year, the heavy maintenance begins.

"Working women are getting into maintenance now. To quit a job when it gets tough is not a good way of coping. Married women can cope this way, at least temporarily, if they choose; and some do. Single women have to hang in there. Or go free-lance. Or start their own firms."

According to the Small Business Administration, business start-ups by women have increased dramatically in the past decade and now account for more than half of all new businesses. Dissatisfaction has obviously driven a lot of women to become entrepreneurs.

Lynne, who moved from one agency to another for ten years before going on her own, says, "I got tired of making some man who didn't appreciate me *rich*. It irritated me. In my last job, the guy who owned the company didn't work nearly as hard as I did; he wasn't very creative. I thought, Why should I put up with all this stuff, get chewed out if a client didn't like an ad, work my ass off to land a new account, put in extra hours when we were swamped—why should I do all this for him?

"Why not for me?

"Going on my own was much easier than I thought it would be. And I love the feeling of control I have now. I can take a day off or work harder if I want more money. It's all up to me. I don't want to grow bigger though. I want to keep it simple, just me working out of my home. Overhead kills small businesses."

Small ad and public relations shops are among the easiest businesses to start—if not the easiest to make thrive. Colleen, too, is thinking about going off on her own. She is dissatisfied with her salary of $21,000 a year. "It's low for someone with my years of experience in PR.

"The gossip on the street is that Allen only hired women (until Randy) because we would work cheap and men wouldn't. The men he interviewed all wanted more money. One of them threatened to sue him for reverse discrimination. He got scared and hired Randy."

When it was time for Colleen's first annual salary review, Allen said he was too busy. He kept postponing the meeting and finally told her she would get a raise, though he didn't have time to tell her how much. "He told me it would show up on my next paycheck."

Allen, not the salary, is the chief source of her job dissatisfaction. "A year ago I told people I was working for the best boss in town. We were a close group, like a family really; and work was fun. He has changed dramatically. I think he's under pressure from the investors to produce; and he has had some disappointments of his own. I don't believe everything has worked the way he thought it would. We moved to bigger quarters, hired a decorator and did it up big when we got the national account. If that goes, he could be in real trouble."

Colleen's dissatisfaction, *women*'s dissatisfaction, is usually expressed in personal terms: "If Allen were the same person he was a year ago when I started, I wouldn't be thinking about leaving now."

Far more than men, we will work for low financial rewards, few tangible benefits—if the psychological benefits are there. We want to feel needed, appreciated; we want to work in a warm, congenial family atmosphere. We worry about upsetting coworkers or bosses just as we would if they were family.

Colleen worries that Jessica may be mad at her if she quits. "Jessica really sees Allen's side in everything. I hope it won't ruin our friendship, especially if I go into business with Anne, which is what I'm thinking about doing."

In spite of all the articles and books telling women how to get ours in the workplace, we still don't. Often we don't even ask for it. Most of us are resigned to the fact that equal pay doesn't exist, that garbagemen make more than nurses. Comparable worth—equal pay for jobs requiring comparable levels of skill, education, experience—has not caught on as a hot political issue.

Why do we still believe it's acceptable for society to value male-dominated professions over female? Why do we not blink when nurses earn less than hospital maintenance workers?

Sheron says, "We gave a seminar on comparable pay and practically no one showed up. The times aren't right for it. Women haven't yet reached the point where they're ready to admit they will have to work all their lives."

The times certainly aren't right for revolution, workplace or otherwise. A fight for comparable pay would be an admission on the part of women that our jobs are as important, as life-long as men's. And comparable pay would change the entire social structure of the country. If secretaries and laborers had the same value to society and received the same pay, male laborers would earn less than they are earning now perhaps, and female data processors more. And the whole concept of man as breadwinner would turn a pile of bread crumbs.

Sheron says, "When we unite for comparable pay we will be forced to face what is already true in America: women too must earn their own living."

Even women to expect to remain single haven't reached the point of assuming full fiscal responsibility—forever.

Kara says, "On the one hand, I know I have to work. I don't see marriage in my future. But I still haven't made the mental leap I should make. And I don't do the same things to build a career as my friend Ned or my brother or men I know.

"In the county offices, the men are automatically promoted just

because they're men. The women, though we outnumber them, go
nowhere. The women might be smarter and work harder, but they
aren't going anywhere. I should get out of there.

"I used to make waves, not about promotions, but about a lot
of things. Nobody really cares very much about their work here. I
used to care. I wanted things done right. Nobody liked me. I was
working so hard to do things right that nobody cooperated; and I
got little done. Everybody made it harder for me to do my job.
Then I was laid off for a while. I came back, in a different position,
which I got through Ned's influence.

"And I'm taking it easy. I'm laid back now. I do what I can, but
I don't get excited. You know it's made an incredible difference;
everyone likes me. They think I'm doing a good job now. I'm doing
less; and everyone says I'm doing a better job this time around."

The lesson she says is: Don't cause trouble. And women have
learned that lesson well.

She rebels in other, less overt ways. Frequently she sleeps late
and clocks in shortly after 9:00 A.M., which "drives the supervisor
crazy," even if she stays late. She takes every medical and personal
day off she has coming.

"But I go in well dressed and smile and get along. I don't argue.
I'm not pushy. Sometimes it still bothers me. Theoretically we're
there to help people; and we could be helping them more than we
are. But nobody cares. And there's nothing I can do about it by
myself. Ironically, I can get more done for my clients by doing less
because no one goes out of their way to slow things down for me.

"I know I should have gone back to school, found a real career
and a way to make good money. Whenever I plan to take courses,
I find an excuse not to do it. I know if I made good money, I would
be absolutely happy about being single. The only time I'm not happy
about it now is when I'm broke, which is too often these days."

But when she's broke, she thinks, "How I can get something out
of a man"—not "Should I go back to school, into business, look
for another job?"

Jillian says, "It's pragmatic to realize that the answers aren't really
out there for us at this point. Women have had so many miscon-
ceptions about work. Back in the early 1970s, we thought we could
all become company presidents or lawyers. It never occurred to us
that all men weren't presidents and lawyers.

"So now we are faced with the truth about work: most jobs aren't exciting, don't pay well, wouldn't fulfill the average twelve-year-old. But it never occurs to us that we, like men, have to make the best of the workplace because we are stuck there. We should, as they do, demand better wages, more benefits.

"The way out for most of us isn't really going back to school or opening our own business. Yes, it is for some. But most of us still can't be presidents, lawyers, or entrepreneurs. That is the bottom line."

Jillian says her job at the plumbing company isn't exciting, but it is "acceptable. I have a fair salary, a good benefit package, and autonomy. I think autonomy is more important than good relations between employer and employee. I've worked in offices where the female staff couldn't sign an invoice or authorize the purchase of a postage stamp—but they were spoken to softly.

"That wears me down. The realities of the workplace do wear you down. I don't think most of us were ready for this. Go back now and read those books that told us how wonderful work would be. They didn't anticipate the dailiness of working. In some jobs dailiness can be as deadly as everyday housewifing. We didn't understand that; we didn't understand a lot of workplaces come with No EXIT signs now.

"The problem is we didn't think we'd have to work. We still don't think we will always have to work. It's easy to accept something if you can tell yourself it won't be forever."

We thought we could choose. In the face of all the mounting evidence to the contrary, most of us still do think we can. The illusion of choice, this belief in a freedom we don't have, is holding us down.

Have most of us ever really wanted the "right" that men have at birth: the right to support themselves all their adult lives? Unless they are independently wealthy, they are born to be yoked to some employer's cart. We think we are not, that we have options we really don't have anymore.

Married women don't have them either. Our married sisters who live in houses purchased before the interest rates went up may well be the last generation of the privileged American woman. Most couples now find two paychecks a necessity. And the traditional family—working dad, housewife mom, and two cute kids—makes up less than 10 percent of our families. From the outside, marriage looks good, secure, economically sounder than it probably is. And we still hold it up as an alternative to permanent working.

Why aren't women more pragmatic about work? It's hard to be pragmatic on your honeymoon. We are still reluctant to leave the honeymoon phase of our marriage with work.

Last spring I spoke to a junior college class in early childhood education taught by a friend. Most of the girls in the class—and they were all girls—planned to be day-care workers. My topic, a topic on which I had frequently written, was the impact of divorce on the child. The girls wanted to talk about the emotional distress of divorce. Some of them already worked as day-care aides; and they eagerly shared their experiences of dealing with divorce through giving children extra hugs.

I told them the greatest, most lasting impact of divorce on the child was economic, not emotional: Divorce made him and his mommy poor. Divorce almost always reduces the standard of living for women and children. It usually does not for men.

Most of the girls were nineteen years old. They planned (a) never to divorce and (b) to rely on that extra cuddling to cure the ills of divorce suffered by children in their care.

I told them day-care workers average $10,000 a year, not enough to support self and child if it comes to that. They weren't worried. After the class, one of the students told me she was a divorced mother, supporting her child and herself on $5,000 a year. I asked her how she did it and why she wanted to become a day-care worker when she badly needed a job that would better equip her to play her role as head of household.

"I love kids," she said. "It's what I want to do. I want to help. If I'm going to work, shouldn't I be doing what I want to do? Besides, I'm sure I'll meet someone and get married again. I want more children of my own someday."

I was shocked that she could still say these things, could view her future in such romantic, idealistic, foolish terms.

Somewhere down the line the romance will go out of her job. And maybe no other romance will come into her life. Perhaps she will go back to school then and train for work in a more financially rewarding field. Or perhaps she will put together a union of day-care workers and help elevate the profession to the status it deserves.

(What, after all, is more important than looking after the nation's children?) Maybe I've met the Mother Jones of child-care workers. I hope so.

Nevertheless, the romance should be going out of many work marriages soon. The woman of course will be burned. How badly she is burned will depend on how much money she earns.

The women I've met who hold jobs with status, power, and money are happier than the ones who don't. If you're going to be disillusioned in marriage, better to be disillusioned behind the wheel of a Mercedes than an old Ford pickup.

Sheron says, "I have a lot more freedom than single low-income women or married high-income women. I am mobile. I can form close ties with men in my profession without a jealous husband wondering what we're really talking about over lunch. I can make my job the focus of my life; and I still have the material things we think we need in the 1980s.

"My life is structured around my job, just as traditional family life has always been structured around the man's job—and still is even if the woman works too.

"The best position in the world is to be single and pretty and well employed. It is no longer chic to be poor. That is the crux of it. And it is not chic to be powerless. No one will look after you. Women can get power through men, in marriage, or through careers. They lose it in divorce. They certainly never get it by holding merely *jobs*."

10

Where Have Our Values Gone?

*When my dreams showed signs
of becoming
politically correct . . .
then I began to wonder.*
—from *The Fact of a Doorframe*
(1985) by Adrienne Rich

Sheron identifies money and power as the "crux of it." They are the new values taken down from a shelf labeled fifties and polished to high luster, the values to which Americans pledged allegiance when they voted for Ronald Reagan. Many women and most men did vote for Reagan. White males went overwhelmingly Republican. Money and power are the twin pillars upon which the traditional white male value system rests.

In the 1960s and early 1970s male and female baby boomers rejected that system. We saw it as a system that did not, possibly could not, encompass everyone. We felt it limited our area of concern chiefly to the nuclear family—and specifically to providing the highest standard of living possible for that little family unit. *Our* concerns were far wider.

We believed in sexual freedom and left-wing political commitment. We did not believe in war; and it is inconceivable that we would have cheered for the troops who invaded Grenada. We believed in women's rights and civil rights, in the right of small nonwhite countries to self-determinism, in the brotherhood of man and the power of sisterhood. We insisted on open communication, sensitivity, and letting it all hang out. Both young men and women accepted values that had been traditionally more "female" than "male."

Those values were very compatible with the single state. Marriage seemed too narrow. It limited the scope of concern and experience. The nuclear family was much too small in size, restricted in membership, tight-assed in philosophy, to contain our love and care.

Where have those values gone?

Underground. The facts of our lives are certainly at variance with the much-balleyhooed return to traditional values of the Reagan era. Americans say they believe in marriage again—though the odds for divorce continue to hover around 50 percent and more people are single now than ever. Americans say they believe in the "traditional" family—though its numbers are continually shrinking. Flying their ultimate belief banner—"I can have it all!"—women are dressing in lace for evening and softer clothes for the office and flaunting their maternity again. Romance and femininity are high style. Michael Korda, author of *Power!* (1975) and *Success!* (1977), has told women that "tears" are "a powerful weapon"—in the office.

Being single and feminist in 1984, I sometimes feel I am walking the streets in miniskirts the day after *Vogue* decreed maxis. Then maxis never really caught on. I remember sitting on the porch steps watching my two-year-old ride his tricycle up and down the driveway the late summer afternoon I read *Vogue*'s thick fall issue on the maxi. When I went inside, I opened my closet and wondered if there was anything I could do to salvage my minis. I decided there wasn't. Further, I decided I didn't care. I feel the same way about the return to traditional values. It is this season's color; and I don't wear the color well. There is no point in doing much to my wardrobe when this too shall pass.

But I wish other women would put down the magazines now trumpeting ROMANCE! SOFT CLOTHES! MARRIAGE! and BABIES!—and examine the truths in the closets of their lives, which are hanging there exactly like dozens of miniskirts with two-inch hems.

Truth: There aren't enough men to go around; and some of us will never marry or remarry no matter how many magazine articles we read on finding men at health clubs or through the classifieds.

Truth: Some of us have waited too long to conceive; and we aren't going to have those babies.

Truth: The overwhelming majority of us have to work now and will have to work for the rest of our lives, married or not.

Even if we want to drop SINGLE! CHILDLESS! and CAREER WOMAN! for MARRIED! PREGNANT! and MOTHER TAKES A LEAVE OF AB-SENCE!—we may no longer have a choice. Our personal values should be shaped around these truths. They should come from the inside of our lives, not be decreed by the same magazines that tell us whether to wear our trousers pleated or cuffed this year. Style dictators don't understand the facts of our lives any more than they know what shape our bodies are in. And where are they getting their divine inspiration, if not from the ruling class, the arbiters of values, who are largely men?

In spite of the gains women have made in the last decade and a half, we are willing now to submit—or rather resubmit—to male values, to the doctrine of male righteousness, which says he is righter than we are and he will determine the course of our lives. Numerous social commentators have cited a lot of reasons for the return to traditional values:

• People are reacting in part to the excesses of the recent past, sexual excesses, the abuse of drugs and alcohol, the excesses of radical feminist rhetoric.

• As women we have been out in the workplace long enough to have become disillusioned and discouraged—to look back longingly at a safer time. (Why else would someone as chic as Lynne surround herself with fifties memorabilia, garish plastic planters, neon-colored Fiestaware dishes, sunburst clocks, plastic statues of Mickey Mouse?)

• The economic recessions of the 1970s made everyone fearful, fearful enough to long for a daddy figure like Reagan at the head of state and a husband in the home, talismans to keep us safe.

• After a period of self-flagellation following the Vietnam War, we longed to feel good about America again, to return spiritually to a traditional national pride.

But there is one motivating factor behind this major value shift from secular humanism to the white man's dollar that the commentators do not mention: *the scarcity of available males.* When any commodity is scarce, it becomes precious; and society builds a cult of desire around it. Is it any surprise that, in the desire to attract and keep one of the few precious men, we have submerged our values of a decade ago and "rediscovered" theirs? If there were few of us and many of them, then *they* would be scrambling to fit into our time schedules, value systems, *lives,* as we now struggle to fit into theirs.

"We wouldn't let them get away with so much," Kara says, "if they were not the ones who make the most money. Money is where it's at today. Most of the men I know are pompous, puffed up little people. I don't know if they are more pompous now than they were ten years ago or if I'm noticing it more. But ten years ago my friends were mostly men. I liked men; and I thought women were largely boring nits. Now I have come full circle, 180 degrees in the other direction.

"I like women better than men. Women know what's going on; they keep things sane.

"Men have changed for the worse. Women are always complaining not only about the quantity of men, but the quality. It's true: Men aren't as good as we are. Maybe it's because we have become more accommodating. They can get away with anything now; and they know it. They act accordingly. Maybe it's because we have had to try harder than they do, be better than they are, to get anywhere.

"Certainly I am more of a feminist now than I was a decade ago. But I am sometimes disappointed in women. I would like us to behave well, in the face of losing odds, not to throw ourselves at men."

Kara's values have "softened," not changed dramatically. She has retained her liberal-left political leanings and voted for Mondale in the last election. So did Jillian and Sheron, though Sheron says, "Part of me was relieved when Reagan won after all. I think it was the part that owns stocks and bonds. I am not proud of that part, but it's there. I could feel good for voting the right way—and also feel good because my interests were being protected. Some people called the election a no-win situation. For me, it was no-lose."

Kara, who meant to campaign for Mondale but never quite got around to doing it, says, "I know a lot of Democrats who voted listlessly. We still believe the same things we believed a decade ago, but we are less zealous. We don't see the point anymore. There's a lot of fat in everything, politics and feminism. We see the fat. I sympathize with the same people I sympathized with a decade ago— the poor, the homeless, the disadvantaged, the victims of racism and sexism—but I am coming from a different position now. I know I have to be making my own way while I am sympathizing with the same beliefs. That makes me less zealous."

Carolyn, the Lawrence, Kansas, mother of two, voted for Reagan. "I am barely struggling by; and I will not vote for anyone who promises to raise my taxes as Mondale did. Besides, I don't believe in welfare. I'm not getting it so why should others? Why should I vote for someone who will take what I have and give it to some woman who doesn't work?

"A friend of mine, a Democrat, a woman who is married to a successful man, told me I am exactly the kind of person who should not vote Republican because I benefited less from the Republican administration than anyone, than she did.

"She got angry at me; and she said I was poor, just too stupid to know it and too proud to admit it. No, I am not poor, not *that* kind of poor."

Nobody wants to be poor. In the 1960s, poverty, of the nouveau temporary variety, was chic. The sons and daughters of lawyers and doctors lived together in college dorms or communes with the sons and daughters of laborers, who were the first in their families to earn college degrees. Everyone wore beads around their necks and flowers in their hair, drank jug wine, smoked pot, and pontificated on the brotherhood of man.

Jillian says, "In those days if one person had money and scored some grass, everyone smoked. We shared. We didn't remonstrate against those who didn't contribute equal amounts of money. I look back at those times and I hardly believe I felt the way I did, so casual about money and possessions. It was wrong to be serious about those things then.

"Now I hide my stash; and I smoke alone. I rarely offer a joint to anyone. I tell myself this is because times have changed and no one smokes anymore. No one, including me, smokes much.

"But I have a feeling we're all smoking what we do smoke alone, because we're just too cheap to share it. That's so funny isn't it? We shared so willingly when we had much less to share."

Kara says, "We gave freely of anything we had, including sex. Now we don't give so freely. We want something for our money. And so do men. Well, men especially do. It's their value system; and we've been working within it long enough to know that's how things are. We can't give too freely anymore, not without feeling like fools."

We can't afford to give freely since we earn less money than men; and we have all accepted the basic tenets of the new faith, which is based on money. A house is no longer a home without cable, a VCR, a microwave, a computer. We, who as children coming of age criticized our parents for their generation's materialism, lust after things they don't find necessary.

Carolyn, who once sewed flower appliqués over the holes on her worn jeans, stood in line for one hour and forty-five minutes at a discount store to get a number that would allow her to come back another day and stand in another line to purchase a cabbage patch kid—if she was lucky and her number got called. She laughs: "It was worse than trying to get into a rock concert. And my number didn't come up."

A generation that once dressed in blue denims that made us indistinguishable from each other have now elevated consumerism to a reason for being. We aren't embarrassed by having or wanting so much. We are only embarrassed by the lack of things.

"If we are going to have things, a lot of things, we need men," Jillian says. "Women don't make enough money. So we have to have them, or we think we do, which is all the same. Men, as husbands, are more important to us now because of money.

"I have a portable TV set at the office; and I watch "Donahue" and "Sally Jessy Raphael" every morning. Raphael did a show on successful men the other day. She was talking about why successful men are lousy lovers. They don't have to try hard, she says, because they think success is enough. They're right. It is.

"At one point, she asked women if they would trade: If they would take $1,000 less from their husband's annual income and get what they considered to be $1,000 more in loving attention from their men.

"A small spattering of hand clapping indicated a few women would trade. Most of those women wouldn't trade. They wouldn't give up even $1,000 of their husband's annual income for more love, sex, affection, whatever.

"That's what men have come to mean to us. We are back almost full circle to the 1950s: You marry a guy so you can have that house complete with all the appliances.

"Watching Raphael's show, I felt sorry for all the husbands out there. But I suppose they have forced the situation on us. They don't want us to have equal pay. They want the power edge; having the edge also means you are dehumanized a little.

"We are dehumanized, but so are they."

The revolutions of the 1960s and 1970s were human revolutions, meant to "humanize" that traditional white male value system, to bring all of us—men and women, black and white, gay and straight—into the system as equal partners. It never quite happened. History is rife with the cycles of revolution and repression, liberalism and conservatism, the halcyon days of Democrats giving way to the halcyon days of Republicans and back again. Americans in particular seem a nation of pendulum swingers.

But some of the changes wrought in social upheaval have endured.

In the aftermath of the sexual revolution, the typical male over twenty-one does not expect his bride to be a virgin. In 1964, my best friend, Gale, was dating a man who insisted on only having anal sex—to preserve her virginity. He would not marry a woman who wasn't a virgin on her wedding day, he told her, even if she had been, as Gale was, a virgin until him, even if they had done everything, which they did, except penetrate her hymen, even if virginity was only a technicality that pleased him. Anal sex hurt; and Gale hated it. In 1985, no man would be able to convince her of the necessity of hurting her rectum to preserve her hymen.

In 1964, I visited a boyfriend at the Naval Air Academy in Pensacola, Florida. Black men wouldn't get on the same elevator as a white woman alone. They hung back and looked at the ground and let the elevator pass. My boyfriend said with satisfaction, "They know their place, not like coloreds in the North." In 1985, that would never happen.

In 1964, I applied for a summer job. The personnel director grilled me about marriage plans, if any. He demanded to know if I planned to use birth control "in the event of sexual activity." And that wouldn't happen today either.

Yet in some ways attitudes are remarkably prerevolutionary.

Women too willingly step back into more submissive roles after a period of stepping out and standing up for ourselves. We went to work in the 1940s while men were at war. Women ran factories, making the planes and tanks, guns and trucks, needed to fight the war. Yet in the 1950s women meekly went back to suburbia, painted their lips bright red, pulled in their waists with long-line bras, and had babies—two, three, four, or more of them. Now after a decade of angry feminism, we are willing again to adapt ourselves to please men.

Now we aren't having four babies and staying home; but they *don't want* four babies and a stay-at-home wife.

They do want their way. Male righteousness is rife in our society. Ryan and I broke up because I could not follow him into the wilderness of his new faith. It was not enough that I learned to accept it, agreed to keep my mouth shut. I had to submit to it. He would not compromise on that. He was sure his life-style was "right" (as he had been sure the way he lived his life before he completely changed it was also right) and every other way of living was "wrong."

I was married to a man who felt the same way about his faith, his politics, his personal habits.

Men have traditionally drawn the lines defining women's lives. We take their names; and their social status according to their job titles and annual salaries is conferred upon us. We assume their faiths, their families, and their friends as our own. And that is different now only for a certain kind of woman, who lives on a certain professional level, earning enough money, commanding enough respect, to keep her own name and determine her own social status. *Any* man has that much power; very few women do. And we accept this status quo.

For the rest of us, marrying up is still the way up. We want men to be older, taller, richer; and they in turn insist we recognize the rightness of their ways. Recently I went on one date with a tax attorney in the six-figure bracket. The following day he called to tell me what I needed to do with my life—all the little adjustments that would make it fit his, including go to bed and get up earlier and send my son to his father's on Friday nights. He was very surprised when I wouldn't even consider complying.

After all: They make more money. We want more things. We will get the money, the power, the things by marrying them. Both sides know that; and knowing gives them the edge.

When we valued men and money less, we valued ourselves and each other more.

An important element common to the antiwar movement and

the early days of feminism was the deep sense of camaraderie among those who shared beliefs. We were creating new life-styles, forging new values; and we were intensely close to each other. We made new relationships beyond the traditional family; and we were often closer to those people than to our own family members. What baby boomer hasn't spent a Thanksgiving or Christmas holiday with friends that stands out in memory as one of the "best," better than family times?

Jillian remembers "a wonderful holiday in Massachusetts with friends. I felt very proud when I contrasted my life to my mother's then. She never had the dining room filled with dinner guests when she could honestly say she liked all or even most of the people there—that they were truly her friends. She gave duty dinners for her family and my father's family and for his business associates. She entertained his friends and their wives; and she rarely liked the wives. Her real friends she saw at lunch or a kaffeeklatsch because my dad didn't like their husbands.

"I always liked the people with whom I broke bread. That seemed to me to be one hallmark of our generation then. We weren't phony. In contrast, our parents were hypocrites.

"We were honest and proud of our honesty. Well, we aren't so honest anymore."

We were *so* honest we said things to our friends our parents never would have said to theirs. We were sure our friendships could stand the stress of all that truth. And for a long time they could and did. But as we changed and grew in different directions, we had trouble making our friendships encompass our differences.

Bonnie, my best friend through my unhappy housewife years, remained my best friend for several years after my divorce. We were friends for fourteen years. And we stopped being friends in large part because she was *very* married and I was *very* single. The friendship ended in 1980, my most successful financial year and the year her younger son entered first grade.

We had a lot of fun together in one of those laughing-through-the-tears kind of friendships that women often have. The strength of it carried us through my divorce, her unwanted pregnancy, which resulted in the difficult birth of a wanted child, and the year her husband spent traveling to Chicago when she needed him at home. It outlasted my love affairs. We lived through all that and then stopped being friends because she thought I bought too many pairs of shoes, and I thought she had too much Tupperware. We were like two men caught in a war of righteous ways.

I thought she should do something, anything other than be a housewife bordering on the agoraphobic who too often whined to her husband, "Do something about the boys. Make them listen to me." I wanted her to get a job. Take a class. Stop playing long-suffering wife, mother, daughter.

She insisted I recognize that her marriage was wildly happy, that they couldn't get enough of each other in bed, that she loved being a mother who indulged her children, a daughter who helped her mother paint and wallpaper a new house. She and her husband touched each other a lot when I was around; but he also flirted with me. Back in our honest days, when I was still married, we had talked about the flirting, the attraction that was never important enough to jeopardize my friendship with Bonnie. When I was single, we didn't talk about ths topic anymore.

We reached a point that also occurs in marriages gone sour: We were bringing out the worst in each other. She had become a whiner; and I had become a nag. We spent a lot of time in the last several months of our friendship discussing her problems, her "insecuri-ties." If her husband was around, and increasingly he wasn't, he read magazines, ignored us and the kids, who were being nasty to each other. In those counterproductive circular chats, we never solved her problems. We succeeded only in staking off our territories and defending them. She was the housewife–martyred mother. I was the working woman.

We both expected me to be tough and uncompromising, just as we expected her to be yielding, warm, an emotional junky.

"I can't live up to your standards," she cried; and I refused to cry.

She never questioned, nor did I, that the growing gulf between us should exist. She was married and dependent; I was single and independent.

The last time we lunched together (until several years later) we fought about where we should eat. "We'll go here because I'm driving," I said like a petulant adolescent with the keys to mama's car. I had the power. "I hate this place," she whined and ordered a salad full of the red onions she hates so she would have good reason to pout.

I missed her for a long time. Yet now I cannot imagine being very close to a married woman, married in the way Bonnie was and still is. I came to believe what happened between us was fated. By 1980, women had lost a sense of solidarity. Or perhaps the solidarity had never really existed; and by 1980, we were forced to recognize this. Women were divided into camps: We were prochoice or prolife, for ERA or against, married or single, feminist or "I'm not a feminist but . . ."

In the heat of the movement, most feminists were not married. Or they were unhappily married, on the verge of divorce, or at least ferociously battling with husbands over the dishes. They were not acquiescent like Bonnie. She was a repudiation of everything I believed; and she made me angry, impatient, intolerant.

Sheron says, "Feminists also were not successful businesswomen in the early days. In the early 1970s, I attended a meeting of a radical feminist group and got a cold shoulder. They were wearing jeans, no bras, hiking boots; and they were angry at everything associated with men. Business was associated with men. I was in business school and already dressing in suits.

"They asked me why I didn't want to do something meaningful, important, like become a rape crisis counselor or a truck driver. I thought they had a lot to learn about power. Women in blue jeans never did have any power. They know this now, don't they?"

We know this now; we have grown up. We have come to accept the importance of power as defined by our society in white male terms. Looking back, feminists were incredibly naive; sitting around in women's centers in our jeans and gauze shirts, discovering that women were abused, physically and sexually, psychically and professionally, and that marriage was unfair. Our anger was fierce and raw. We had grown accustomed to fighting injustice, on the picket lines in the civil rights movement, against the war in Vietnam, in situations where right and wrong were clearly defined. This time the injustice was personal, ours alone. Our male compatriots weren't in this fight; in fact, they were the enemy.

But unless we were separatist lesbians, it wasn't that simple. Never before had "they" and "we," the opposing factions, tried to share beds. We were confused; they were confused. And women who sided with men, like Bonnie, only seemed to make life more difficult for us.

Friendships between women, like-minded women, were very important in those days. An independent woman didn't cancel plans with female friends for a last-minute date with a man. Now, years after we have called a truce in the hostilities, we understand if one of our friends does cancel in favor of a man. She doesn't have to lie. We need them more and each other less. We even understand why she doesn't want to introduce him to us. We can't be trusted to leave him alone.

Early into Lynne's new relationship, she told me, "We'll only be able to get together for lunch now. I have to keep my evenings open in case he has time to see me." And before I met him at her holiday open house, she asked me not to wear a sweater dress and not to flirt with him.

When he was talking to me, he saw her watching and said, "Look, she's jealous." Then he leaned toward me and put his hand on my back. "She'll be over any moment," he whispered in my ear. And she was. Putting a proprietary arm around him, she asked me, "So, what's going on?"

I hadn't played that scene since my young married days, ten, twelve, fifteen years ago. What's "going on" is that women have changed. So have men. They're smarter now. He set her up; and she performed on cue. She did not ask *him*, "What's going on?" As women have traditionally done, she blamed it on a woman.

"I think everything that's happened to us in the 1980s is tied up with the failure of ERA," Jillian says. "A lot of women stopped trying in the early 1980s when it became obvious we were not going to get the amendment. When they stopped trying and pushing so hard for change, they became more accommodating to men. But that was only part of it.

"I think women also realized they weren't accomplishing anything by being very aggressive. Look at the winners: Phyllis Schlafly and her Eagle Forum contingent working their female ploys, winning through playing up to and manipulating men. Schlafly is a manipulator extraordinaire. She has no shame. She got what she wanted; and we only succeeded in alienating men.

"It was like a light came on in a million women's heads at the same time; and they knew this stage was over.

"The defeat of ERA closed a chapter on feminism just as Kent State closed the books on the 1960s. We lost some idealism with each closing. It's amazing that people who came of age in the 1960s, witnessing the three major assassinations on television, that these people would have any idealism left at all, isn't it? You would have thought we'd have been very cynical, very young. It took a lot to make us cynical. Kent State didn't do it, not for women. ERA finally did it.

"Politics were no longer personal to me after that. They were just politics. Yes, I vote Democratic, but I don't have a whole lot of faith in the party's ability to get anything done. I don't have much hope resting on my vote, like I once did."

The failure of ERA did change attitudes, ours and men's.

Sheron says, "It affected not only our politics but our sense of sisterhood. We no longer could believe we were united when it was so obvious we weren't. Men didn't defeat the Equal Rights Amendment. Women did—largely married women. I remember despising Schlafly and her coterie of radical wives in a way I never despised anyone before. How could that battle not have separated this generation of women as painfully as the Civil War separated a previous generation of people? How could it not have convinced men our 'equality' was questionable?"

I interviewed Schlafly for King Features Syndicate shortly after her rousing victory over her own sex. Driving to her big stone home on the bluffs overlooking the Mississippi River in Alton, Illinois, I was torn with conflicting feelings. I wanted to hate her in person as I'd hated her at a distance. On the other hand, part of me wanted to be a good little girl who would win her approval as if it were Bible verse cards awarded for good behavior on Sunday morning.

She affected women that way: Not only did she polarize groups of women, she successfully polarized the two women each of us is inside. The independent woman rejects her and the value system she upholds. But the dependent woman, the fearful twin who believes that barefoot and pregnant are safe, would like to please Mrs. Schlafly because Mrs. Schlafly speaks for men.

We would not have hated her so much had she not been able to reach the fearful woman inside, had she not spoken for men.

Before our last lunch Bonnie and I had argued about ERA and Phyllis Schlafly. She didn't think we needed a special amendment; and she thought Schlafly was correct in assuming it would "force women out of the home." Bonnie refused to believe economic realities were already "forcing" most women out of their homes.

Now, Bonnie drives a school bus, a job she considers expendable ("though we do spend the money," she laughs). And I'm sure she still wouldn't see the need for ERA.

The great difference between us is that she cannot really believe in the possibility of being alone, of having to support herself and her sons, of having to take her own car to the garage. Marriage has preserved her innocence, her air of housewifely "niceness." She is proud that she can't say no to any request, whereas I am proud that I can. She feels the politics of the 1980s validate her.

The difference drove a wedge into our friendship. But we weren't alone. The same thing was happening to other women, other sets of female friends.

"There's no doubt the defeat of the amendment helped to increase the acceptance of a male value system again," Kara says. "A lot of women who were sitting on the fence about feminism looked at our defeat and saw we couldn't deliver. The strength was still with men and women who worked through them. Schlafly is the all-time great at playing the male game while speaking in an acceptably female way. Even if you hate her, you have to recognize her power. Losing ERA reinforced the message: Women's values don't make it in the real world.

"Feminism has become of necessity a quiet movement of late."

Colleen echoes that opinion: "There is a big difference in the way more active feminists move in the world now and the way they moved in, say, 1976. ERA is part of it. But things were changing before then, as soon as we *smelled* defeat.

"Generally, women are less militant, even the women you would expect to be militant, the high achievers, public figures. I'll bet if you did a study you would find nowhere near as many sex discrimination lawsuits filed last year as in 1976—and we have not put an end to discrimination.

"Women are more into manipulating within the system—or else they are passive. Everyone is more power-oriented; and we know you don't get power by suing your employer. You'll never work there again. Maybe you'll never work anywhere else either. You don't gain power in lawsuits; all you gain is notoriety and a martyr's label."

In her previous job, Colleen knew she was paid thousands of dollars less than a male colleague with nearly identical credentials who'd held the same job for almost the same amount of time.

"But I didn't do anything about it. The salary discrimination was documented in personnel files. It had been admitted by the CEO, the personnel director, and my supervisor. They all said my male coworker asked for a bigger starting salary than I did. I priced myself too low; and they took me at my price.

"I found a memo in my file from the CEO dated shortly after I was hired, saying this matter should be 'rectified immediately.' But it wasn't. Eventually they told me they would 'adjust the difference' by giving me larger pay increases than he received. They said they would remedy the situation, but they couldn't afford to do it all at once.

"I was mad enough at one point to talk to a lawyer. But I didn't follow through. Everyone told me it would hang around my neck forever if I made trouble. So the company continued paying him more, while we did the same job. And I didn't make any trouble.

"That's how women are now. We're smart enough to know we're being had. And it's partly our fault we are. I didn't sell myself very well when I took the job. I didn't ask for enough money. As long as we don't value ourselves as much as they do, we will be underpaid. They aren't going to look after us and give us a fair wage if we aren't clever enough to look after ourselves.

"It all comes down to this: Men value being men. We don't value being women *enough*."

Jillian adds: "We used to talk a lot about everybody being persons, not men and women. But we are again moving like *women* in the world. We are careful of them again.

"Nora Ephron still says it best: All that came out of the women's movement is the Dutch treat. Though we earn less, we are expected to pay our way. Women who think marriage will allow them to quit work are kidding themselves. Men expect wives to work, and to do everything else, and to behave like women.

"Men expect the same superwoman in business. They don't want to pay us equally, but they want equal work from us.

"And incredibly, women do this. What bothers me now is our passive compliance. No one is even shocked when you discuss outright discrimination in salary. No one says 'This is awful' anymore."

And Kara says, "We recently got raises at work. The counselors, who are all women, got smaller percentage increases than the supervisors, who are all men with the exception of two. Several years ago this didn't happen. Everyone got the same percentage increase. In those days, women *demanded* that. Now women don't even speak up. We have slipped back a lot and nobody notices. Are we all too busy doing our nails now or what?

"Some women who do talk about the discriminatory practices blame the Reagan administration; and I'm sure it deserves some blame. But we have to remember who allowed the Reagan administration to steamroll right over us: We did.

"We haven't protested anything since 1980, have we? It was a bloodless conservative coup."

And why don't we protest?

A decade ago we weren't afraid to make men angry at us. Now we are. We have seen that men have power and powerful women are more likely than not aligned with men, or with a man. Ronald Reagan didn't create this situation. He is only the visible symbol, the personification of a particular set of values that the majority of Americans espouse—though, ironically, few of us, including Reagan, live.

Our first divorced president, Reagan and wife Nancy have come to symbolize the traditional marriage. Although he didn't see his granddaughter by adopted son Michael until the child was twenty months old and the lapse had been noted by the press, Reagan preaches traditional family values. The majority of Americans, who have also been touched by divorce and may have children, grandchildren, nieces, or nephews they seldom if ever see, accept these contradictions willingly. We don't want to think; we just want to be reassured. And who wants to see a seventy-year-old emperor without his new clothes?

Like Walter Mondale in 1984, those of us who would prefer to face the facts are fighting a battle of image against reality. The image is comforting; the reality is not.

Society has decreed marriage "in"—though there are 8 million more single women between the ages of twenty and fifty-nine than men, women who won't marry because they *can't* find marital partners. Society values children, yet unpaid child support has become a national disgrace. Increasingly, living in a female-headed household is associated with poverty. And women have let the married and pregnant thirty-three-year-old yuppie in her maternity business suit serve as the media image for all of us—though most of us are concerned about financing the groceries this week, not locating an English nanny.

"Because we are living in a time of such skewed values," Sheron says, "it's really difficult to be a feminist today. Ten years ago we had much more to fight against, but we had the value system of an entire generation behind us. This is the first period of history I can remember in which caring for the underdog is *not* the thing to do.

"For instance, I hear people making disparaging remarks about bag ladies—which would never have happened in the 1960s and 1970s. We would have been outraged about these women being on the streets, sleeping in bus stations. Now we make humorous remarks to each other and move around them, careful not to touch, as if they were catching.

"Everybody seems to have adopted that brittle, shallow sensibility that I have come to associate with the gay culture on the East and West coasts. I don't mean to put down gays. They have developed their particular brand of humor and world view because they have been ridiculed and reviled throughout history. They are defensively offensive.

"But now this viewpoint is chic. I have a very good gay friend who swears to me people wouldn't sleep in paper boxes outside buildings in New York City if they didn't 'prefer that life-style.' He's sure they could go 'someplace' if they didn't 'insist upon being iconoclasts.' It's very funny, but he could say the same thing to a right-wing Republican; and as long as the right-winger didn't know he slept with men, they would see eye to eye.

"How the hell did we get to this point? When we finally got cynical we really got there. But the cynicism is so covert. It wears a three-piece suit and waves an American flag. The most cynical people I know would tell you they are idealistic—about big business, the country, their relationships.

"People keep telling me the TV soap 'Dynasty' symbolizes the new myths of the culture. I have only seen an episode or two. Supposedly everyone who is everyone has switched from 'Dallas' to 'Dynasty' because it has everything: glitz, money, big business, homosexuality to titillate the masses, a powerful male, a manipulating bitch female, and a complete lack of regard for any values except the Carrington family's mania for their own name. Success is a state of grace.

"If 'Dynasty' is where we're all aspiring to be, I suppose we can't expect feminism or any civil rights movement to flourish. The values climate is all wrong.

"We are simply never outraged anymore—unless someone puts the touch on our wallets. You can't have social progress without outrage."

Perhaps we are afraid to be outraged on anyone else's behalf. We don't like to consider how close we may be to the bag lady on the street. When magazines do features on single women, they invariably focus on successful "career" women, not women like Carolyn, who earn a little more than $5 an hour or even women like Kara, in modest dead-end jobs. With no man standing between us and the streets, our security is tenuous—based entirely on those inadequate salaries, on our continued health, on our job security. We can't afford to be outraged by poverty anymore—because poverty is too *possible* for each of us. And we don't think about that possibility.

Lynne, who is not interested in social welfare issues, insists, "I'm not uninterested out of subconscious fear. It won't happen to me. I'm just uninterested.

"I vote Democratic; and I thought it was awful, depressing, that Reagan won so big. But I don't think about the issues very much unless there is an election. I'm so busy. And I don't think of myself as a feminist, not at all. I don't need all that. I was for the Equal Rights Amendment. Well, it was so obvious. It should have passed."

Yet Lynne says she has no problems with the prevailing value system. "Money is power. I like money. And I am attracted to men now who have power. I have learned there are certain things you put up with if you're involved with this kind of superaggressive successful man. It will always be his way. He will never have as much time for you as you would like. I have to get used to that. He's not the kind of man I picked in the past, but look at the mistakes I made in the past."

Though Lynne doesn't identify herself as a feminist, she lives a life that is run in many ways on feminist principles. A hard negotiator in the professional arena, she commands top fees for her creative services. She has a large support system of friends, including men and women. Yet she has a history of allowing men to run the relationships, of valuing the man over everything else in her life. She has traveled widely, on her own and in the company of friends. And she only sees her therapist twice a month now.

I have come to regard Lynne as the litmus-test woman, a paradox, a wealth of conflicting values and images, opposing strengths and viewpoints. She could be plunked right down in the middle of *Time* or *Newsweek* and labeled "Typical New Woman." She is that kind of political bellwether.

But she is not as shallow as she would like to be.

The ability to be shallow in a certain way is valued in the 1980s. We have to have everything, so we can't afford to spend too much passion on any one thing. The only extreme we will tolerate is workaholism. We have created a whole set of psychological symptoms around "alienation," which is only the natural consequence of being shallow. Men and women are "alienated" from each other, from self, from everything but jobs and possessions.

Lynne has affected the attitude: bright, brittle, shallow.

My friend Rob gave me the perspective on shallow and made me realize my litmus-test woman is not really shallow at all. She only appears to be living on the fringes of everything at once.

Rob returned to Edwardsville a year ago because he hated San Francisco, where he had moved in part because he was tired of being alienated in New York: "I didn't want to end up like the people I knew in the gay crowd. They were really shallow. Bright, witty, entertaining, but shallow. I worried I would never accomplish anything. I would spend the rest of my life just talking. Well, I wanted to come back to the Midwest where people led real lives and have real values, where a basic house doesn't cost $200,000 yet.

"I wanted to come home where, as corny as it sounds, you can still divide people into those who have good hearts and those who don't."

The women in this book have those "good hearts."

"I think there is enormous goodness in women," Jillian says. "It bubbles up inside women whenever they are involved with or touched by others. Unfortunately, the companion stream that bubbles up, this need for dependence, exists too. What we have to learn is how to be good without being dependent, caring without becoming earth mother and Christian daughter, loving without being subservient. I believe we will learn, because I believe in women.

"Right now all those baby hormones are making women temporarily mushy in the head. Women—*single* women—*will* lead the next revolution because we have not been protected, we have not completely sold out, we have not lost touch with all our values. Being single keeps us on course."

Kara and I frequently talk about women, when we aren't bitching about men. We talk about the foolish ways in which women, ourselves included, behave—mostly in regard to men—and yet we admire women's goodness, strength, endurance, stability. And most often we are talking about single women, who still, to us at least, seem braver, leaner, and meaner than married women.

"I really don't have many married women friends," she says. "Women's values become so different when they marry. In friendships with them, you have to bend. They will expect you to see them when it's convenient for their husbands or they will invite you over presumably because you are so lonely; and their little homes are such bright beacons. You feel like you should be grateful for the attention, the time they have spared.

"Some conflict between married and single cannot be avoided. They can't support single women too much. Being single might look too good if all other things are equal. They want to maintain the status quo. Married women are aware of their desired social status; and they want to continue having it, especially the ones who have little else."

More of my friends are married than are Kara's. Never marrieds have less understanding of the married state. Formerly marrieds can understand both sides. But I know a truce must exist between a single woman, her married friend, and the ever-present, if invisible, husband. The single woman should not give him any reason to distrust her, to believe she is fomenting domestic rebellion behind his back. This should not be true, but it is: The ties between women are weakened when a man stands in the middle.

Kara and I are close in part because no significant male in either of our lives comes between us. We have the kind of friendship women realized women should have a decade ago. And we lead the kind of lives we thought we should be leading too—only poorer. We have talked about almost everything, but the one thing we never discuss is how we can have it all.

Obviously, we don't. Furthermore, we don't believe we, or most women, can.

The chief value of the 1980s is expressed in this phrase: "having it all." It has replaced "looking out for number one" as a generational tag line. It is the most male of male values. Women have never had it all. Now we think we can.

"All" combines money and power, business and babies, marriage and career, sex and racquetball. And single women are left out by definition. Yet we lust after "all," tantalized by the quotes of celebrities, successful businesswomen, the promises of magazines that sell us everything from products to life-styles on the strength of its allure.

The paradox: Why do we invest so much in questing for a myth beyond our reach? And if this life-style were beyond the reach of so many men, would it still be the cherished myth of our times?

11

The Myth of "Having It All"

The dilemma of the postfeminist woman is that there are only twenty-four hours in a day, and she needs forty-eight to get done all the things she wants to get done, and must still find time to sleep, one hopes not alone.
—Erica Jong in an interview with the author

By the time *Cosmopolitan* editor Helen Gurley Brown wrote *Having It All* in 1982, the phrase was, in our collective consciousness, to happiness as a Rolls-Royce is to automobile. Having it all separates the wife from the single woman—who can seldom afford a Rolls. Brown told us, "Any woman can have a man . . ." A career. Children. Fashionable clothes. Beauty. Time to whip up those elegant little dinners for two right after working out at the gym. And we believed her.

Or rather it was not so much that we believed her, but that she believed us and spouted back in her typical, gushy, breathless, italicized fashion exactly what we wanted to hear. We wanted, and *deserved,* everything. To settle for less, to expect less, seemed like the treason of our times.

In May 1979, *Ms.* magazine was insisting we could have it all when they ran an article by Barbara Ehrenreich, "Is Success Dangerous to Your Health?" debunking the "myth of tension at the top." No, they assured us, "tension at the top" won't kill us, so go for it. (In a sidebar we were told how to cope by letting off steam, etc.) They were as adamant about denying the negatives of the workplace as they were in refusing to admit abortion had its downside.

Three years later, in the August 1982 tenth-anniversary issue, Gloria Steinem said women should resolve in the 1980s to "retire

145

Superwoman." In a resolution that sounded only slightly more re-alistic than the idealistic euphemisms Helen Gurley Brown offered the "mouseburgers" (shy women) of the world, Steinem said:

> This decade may not solve that problem, but it can:
> 1. Finally do away with the idea that one woman can or should Do It All. (Giving up this impossible goal will have the healthy impact of turning guilt into anger and action.)
> 2. See to it that men become self-sufficient. (He who eats can also cook.)
> 3. Reconcile women to the fact that, if we don't do the house-work it won't be done the way we like it. (And that's okay.)

Our magazines generally concede now that Superwoman is, or should be, dead. But a contradiction remains. They still tell us we can have it all. For women, having it all means doing it all. (We have yet to find a way to make men read and accept the resolutions our magazines print.) And surprise, we have just defined Super-woman: the woman who has it, does it all. She is the embodiment of the feminist mystique, as the happy housewife, her mother, em-bodied the feminine mystique.

We are supposed to do it all without sweating in public (as southern belles were once expected to look cool and dry wearing layers of clothing). We are supposed to make "all" look easily acquired. The magic is still performed offstage, as women's magic has always been.

Why would a generation that cut its teeth on Betty Friedan replace the feminine mystique, the happy housewife, with the feminist mys-tique, she who has eight arms and minimal sleep requirements, she who has it all? We took the mythical happy housewife as if she were a department store manikin, removed two, perhaps three, of her four children, added a briefcase, exchanged her long-line bra for a leotard and tights—and called her liberated woman. Now she need not be perfect in one area, but in several areas all at once.

I interviewed so many women in the late seventies and early eighties who described themselves in manikinlike detail. They were the aggressively "happy" halves of two-career couples. My favorite remains Dr. Susan Nelson, a department head at a large eastern state university.

She asked me to call her "Dr. Susie" because "everyone" did.

And she was proud that the plants in her office were kept alive by her own hand. When I met her in 1980, Dr. Susie, age thirty-nine, was hugely pregnant with her second child. Her ankles were swollen; she looked like she needed a nap.

But she droned on about her "life-style": Husband "helped" at home; eighteen-month-old daughter walked and talked; sitter was a "find, a treasure." As she told me about her day in exhausting detail, I wanted to stick a pin in her to see if she would bleed.

What made "the New Woman" behave this way?

One of the same old reasons: guilt. Women are always apologizing for our existence in some way. "Forgive me," our behavior begs, "for being." Our magazines fuel our guilts with articles challenging us to root out our trouble spots, be they on our psyches or our thighs, and fix them. Our television talk shows examine our guilts. Women are forever guilty, for not being whatever it is we should be at the moment, and thus we are forever ripe for the tyranny of the ever more accomplished role model.

But the New Woman also operates out of simple greed, the same greed that motivates men. Why should we not have everything? We grew up as the most privileged children in the history of a country whose founding fathers included "the inalienable right to the pursuit of happiness" in the Constitution. *We* certainly meant to pursue our right to the fullest.

So the late 1970s gave us a new role model: the overachieving woman.

A wife and mother, she was a corporate vice-president or perhaps a lawyer who had earned her law degree after the birth of her sixth child. She was lean and tanned, an expert tennis player who baked her own bread "just for fun." And of course her friends, whose numbers were legion, were wild about her.

She was a Stepford wife with an income of her own.

The real women I knew fell into two categories: those who depended on their husbands; and those who didn't depend on their husbands or had no husbands on whom to depend.

The dependent wives talked about their newly diagnosed cases of hypertension and popped tranquilizers. They developed midlife allergies and gained a lot of weight. And they had a million excuses for why they could let one course at a state university consume their lives.

The nondependent women earned money and grew mold on the leftovers in their refrigerator. Their ovens never had to be cleaned. They went to work many mornings with the hems of their suits taped in place.

The common denominator between both groups was guilt. Dr. Susie shamed us all. But at least she gave us something in common: Guilt was the only thing we shared with each other and our mothers.

Our mothers were guilty when their floors didn't shine, their cookies burned on the bottoms. When they weren't happy. What a simple life!

We were guilty when our Cuisinarts gathered dust, our hips gathered fat, our children caught colds in day-care centers. We felt like failures because we weren't corporate VPs or didn't have multiple orgasms on demand. When we weren't happy all the time.

Because of guilt, women have created a virtual cult of self-improvement. Men may worry about their bodies more now than they did twenty years ago—but which sex buys books such as *Thin Thighs in Thirty Days*? Look at the magazines displayed on newsstands and read the cover blurbs.

In the space of one typical month, *Playboy* (March 1985) was selling "What Makes 60 Minutes Tick?" and *Esquire* (February 1985) pushed an issue devoted largely to "success." Women's magazines offered: "5 Amazing Thigh Makeovers (from Jiggles and Flab to Toned and Sexy in Just 12 Weeks)" in *Glamour* (February 1985), "The New You!" and "Firm Fanny Guide" in *Harper's Bazaar* (February 1985), and "What Smart Women Know about the Man Hunt" in *Cosmopolitan* (February 1985).

So which sex considers having it all a moral imperative to create personal perfection—and which sex figures having it all means earning enough money to buy it?

As an achievable goal, having it all is the ultimate triumph of image over reality in a society hooked on image. It is all about not making choices, which is why it appealed to us baby boomers so much.

Single women split on many issues, depending on whether they are never marrieds or formerly marrieds, but on this one issue, the possibility of having everything, the split seems to be determined by age.

"The younger you are," Jillian says, "the more you think it's still possible to marry Mr. Right, have two perfect children, one boy, one girl, and be president of the company before age forty. Then, as you get closer to forty, you begin to think, 'No, all these things aren't possible.' That is the real midlife crisis: coming to terms with what is actually possible versus what is totally outside the range of possibility."

Colleen, who is only thirty, still believes she can and will have everything. "Of course I haven't given up on the idea of marriage! And I do want children, whether I marry or not. But I don't think I will have to make the choice of being a single mother; I think I will marry. I'd like to take some time out, maybe work part time for a few years when the children are babies—but I don't see losing my career over motherhood.

"Yes, I want everything and I think I will have it."

Her friend Jessica, at thirty-seven, says, "Women *should* be able to have it all, but I don't honestly think it's possible anymore. Eric will never understand my children; and if we get married he wants a baby of his own. I can't decide now if that's a good idea, since I'm about ready to kill the two I have. My son has been getting detention several times a week for the past few weeks. I have to leave work early to pick him up and then be late for meeting Eric. Yesterday he said 'fuck' to a teacher.

"And Dawn isn't getting any better. Things at work aren't going well. Maybe some women have it all, but I don't know how they do it. I don't have it all. I'm beginning to think I can't. Right now I would be happy if everyone wasn't always mad at me."

Colleen, who is also irritated with Jessica because "she cries all the time," can't understand her "inability to create a balance between love, work, and kids. Why is she so all or nothing? Why can she only concentrate on one area at a time? I sympathize with her unhappiness, but I don't understand the way she manages her life."

I can understand because Jessica and I were part of the first-line troops in the Superwoman corps. The front line always takes the worst hits while the rear guard figures out how to fight a war.

Jessica has been told—and she fervently believes—she should excel in all areas of her life all at once: work, love, motherhood. But she had no training, no role models to show her *how*.

Pragmatically, Kara says, "The only way any woman has it all is to marry money, a man who can help her buy it all. Even if she works, she needs more than her salary to pull it all off. Having it all is our generation's version of the good life. And it always takes money to buy domestic help, meals out, vacations, electronic gadgets."

But the one thing Kara envies about married women is their ability, if they have married well, to have it all.

And the one thing Jessica feels most guilty about now is her inability to pull it all off.

And the one thing Colleen is sure she will manage to do is have it all.

The image is that strong, the myth that potent. To turn your back on "all," or the tantalizing possibility of someday having it, is like saying, "No, thank you, I never really wanted multiple orgasms in the first place."

"I think it is the one big reason we envy married women," Jillian says. "They at least have the potential for living the myth. We don't. Maybe their marriages are lousy and their kids impossible. Maybe their family responsibilities have held them back in their careers. Maybe they hate their jobs, but they can't afford to quit any more than we can.

"But we look at them and we see a *Redbook* cover come to life.

"It's very important to live up to society's image of the ideal woman. Each society has one. In our society, the image keeps getting tougher to achieve. All Scarlett O'Hara had to do was learn how to take shallow breaths after she was laced into her corset.

"On the other hand, no wonder she got into so much trouble. She was bored. Look at what women have to do today. And I really don't think they understand they're still not free. I don't think they step back and see the truth, how much they are trapped inside a marketing concept. Single women have at least a good chance of seeing this, because we are on the outside looking in.

"Married women are too caught up in the competition."

The writer Virginia Woolf said, "I thought how unpleasant it is to be locked out; and I thought how it is worse perhaps to be locked in." She wasn't specifically talking about marriage, but she could have been.

As soon as I got divorced, I was out of the Superwoman sweepstakes. I was a person with no clearly defined status. I had lost the status of my former husband. I was locked out of the society of middle-class couples. It *had* been worse to be locked in.

My new profession, writer, had panache that extended beyond the limits low income placed on me. The wives of high-priced attorneys took me to lunch at the country club. Although it's true they didn't invite me to couples dinners, I also did not have to give those dull little parties in return. I haven't played hostess since people were dipping chunks of rye bread into the beau monde dip; and I am glad.

"Being single has its privileges," Jillian says. "The best one is not having to do everything to maintain one's status in life. I watch married women knocking themselves out to keep everything together; and I think they're crazy."

Sheron agrees: "Nobody can have everything all at once, even if it looks like they do on the surface. You can't convince me men have or ever had it all either. Sure they've had marriages, kids, careers, and it all hung together because they had full-time wives to manage the details—*but* has the twelve-hour-a-day executive ever had time to enjoy his family and all the goodies his money buys? Has he really had everything or just paid for it?

"I think I have a more comfortable, enjoyable life than people who try to have everything. Single women are more likely to be aware of the discrepancy in myth and reality than married women. I think married women have to invest a lot in believing they have it all; and we don't.

"I have watched several married women now try to keep it all together. Usually the addition of a second child is the finishing touch. Everything collapses. They have to cut back their hours at work or find a less demanding job. Grandma stops baby-sitting because the new baby has colic. The first child, now three, has adjustment problems.

"These women are always profoundly shocked when anything goes wrong. They are the first generation of mothers who expected foolproof kids. They are so overscheduled they can't possibly handle one small problem.

"I mentored a woman last year who spent most of the six months following her baby's birth crying. She had trouble with the sitter. Leaving the baby every morning upset her. If she didn't cram her briefcase full of work at night she felt guilty. Then if she didn't get the work done, she felt guilty. She asked me why it was so hard for her when it was so easy for everyone else.

"She really believed it was easy for everyone else. She accepted the visuals in the slick magazine layouts. She read the articles that say, 'Oh, you're having a little problem? Here's how you solve it, one, two, three.'

"I took her an article I found in the *New York Times Magazine* this year about career women who have decided to take time out or work part time because they are exhausted from juggling marriage, kids, job. She was so relieved to find she wasn't alone.

"I can't imagine what she would have done as a single mother. I don't know how they cope."

Single mothers are the unsung supermoms.

How many of them chose to have babies out of wedlock because they were seduced by the myth of having it all? How many of them felt (as Lynne says she sometimes does) they wanted to "experience" motherhood—and then discovered motherhood is not an "experience" in the same way an affair, a bottle of French wine, a trip to Italy, is an experience? What a shock it was to all of us, married or single, to discover that children really do not lie quietly in their cradles waiting for quality time. How did single mothers survive that shock alone?

Gerri, Jillian's single-mother friend, says, "Coping with that shock wasn't as hard as you might think. Really, I was more prepared for the downside of motherhood than the married yuppies I know. A single woman goes through so much soul-searching before she gets pregnant. A married woman only has to decide one thing: Does she want a child now or not?

"What did surprise me was the reactions of people in my age group. I thought they, who want to have everything for themselves, would understand my deep need for a child too. They might have if I had adopted rather than conceived. Buying what you want is acceptable always. But putting yourself through pregnancy and birth alone is a little raw for yuppie sensibilities. I wonder if they would give birth at all if babies could be bought like Cabbage Patch Kids."

Gerri calls having it all the "yuppiest value"; yet she says "I felt more yuppie when I was going for it, when I was making up my mind to get pregnant and not deny myself motherhood because I was single, than I have felt since I got closer to achieving it. Now it looks like I have or almost have everything I want. But I would tell anyone it isn't really possible.

"Now I understand *prices*. You pay for everything. My generation thinks you always pay in money; and that isn't true. The cost, the real cost, is more than money. It's time, energy, love, your soul. And that is the real reason no one can have it all."

Having it all is a value embraced by yuppies precisely because it *does* require a steady flow of cash, an ever-increasing credit line. At the same time, "all" places a high value on individual achievement. Having it all requires the right mix of guilt and greed: more greed in the male mix, a higher percentage of guilt in the female mix.

"Yuppies don't just buy; they also do," Sheron says. "They are goal-oriented achievers. The unemployed wife of a wealthy man for instance can never really have it all.

"This value expresses the most you can do and be and have—the height of accomplishment. It has become a very effective marketing pitch. It's interesting that the person responsible for the Michelobe Light beer pitch—'You *can* have it all'—is a woman."

(Susan Gilette, senior vice-president/group creative director at Chicago ad agency Needham Harper Worldwide, a thirty-four-year-old married mother of two, has been described by the *Chicago-Tribune* as "the embodiment of the ideas communicated by the Michelobe Light campaign." And she insists, "You can have it all if you don't sleep much.")

Sheron says, "The implication of the beer ads, and the coffee generation spots too, is that this new breed is living each area of life to the fullest. Well, anyone who is truly committed to the corporate success path knows this is not possible.

"The corporation demands too much of fast trackers. You can reach a certain level of success, the mid-level, which is all most people reach anyway, and still have time for other things. If you go farther, you can't get there without sacrifice, without slighting the other things in your life.

"And what's wrong with that? Why are we not supposed to make choices anymore? I would rather live intensely on one level than dabble in several levels."

Yet most of us made the choices we did a decade ago precisely because we thought we did not have to choose "one level" on which to live "intensely." We did not marry men who were less than absolutely everything a man should be. Or we left men who did not make us 100 percent happy. We refused to settle, to make any choice that permanently eliminated having it all.

Carolyn says, "I thought my marriage was a compromise. And I honestly did not think I should have to compromise."

Jillian says, "I have never found a man who wouldn't have been a compromise of some sort; and I have never wanted to compromise."

Kara says, 'I have never been ready to compromise."

Lynne says worriedly, "I shouldn't settle, should I? Sometimes I think I'm going to settle. No one should."

And I felt the same way. When I left my husband, I wasn't 100 percent happy, not 90 percent, 80 percent, 70 percent. I don't know what the percentage was, but it certainly wasn't high enough for a daughter of the 1960s, who grew up believing in the possibility of making straight A's right through life.

Being single has forced me to admit one really cannot keep an A average going throughout life. I don't know how much longer I would have kidded myself into believing it was *possible*—possible, and I wasn't doing it!—had I remained a wife. For several years after my divorce, I listened with growing irritation to my married friends talk. Some had careers and were talking about having babies too. Some had children and were planning to go back to work. They were all sure it was possible to have everything.

I thought they irritated me because I was jealous of them. Then I knew they irritated me because they were fools. The truth is we can't have everything, not all at once. Single women slam up against this hard reality sooner than married women; and we are lucky we do.

If we could just see their lives in the same harsh light as we are learning to see our own, we would be even luckier.

Because we have been told that a good marriage is a significant part of "all," we forget *any* marriage is not necessarily a good marriage. Many women are locked in a state of emotional isolation that is actually far lonelier than being single. Living on the outside, we too often look into the portholes of their marriages and see Hallmark card families where none exists.

I remember leaving Bonnie's house and feeling so alone because she and her husband stood together framed in the lighted doorway, their arms around each other, waving good-bye in unison, while I went out into the dark, the cold—alone.

But I would not have had Bonnie's husband, or her neuroses, on a bet. I do not have one married friend whose husband I covet. In fact, I do not have a married friend whose husband I would have on loan for a week. Maybe those of us who chose to be alone a decade ago no longer have this choice—but neither do our married sisters. And they are living with those men we would not have, still feeling obligated to have it all.

Growing up ultimately means accepting some limits and making some choices. That we have persisted in thinking the options are limitless as long as we have says something about our generation. Maybe some of us will not grow up until we are fifty, sixty, seventy—and have to admit we cannot choose *not* to die.

Recently Rob accused, "But you have it all: an interesting career, a handsome, charming son, a good body, and a sex life. You have everything you really want except money."

I told him what I have, and have had, is almost all, the closest one can really come to nirvana.

For the first five years of my son's life I was mostly his mother; and the only thing I regret about that period of my life now is the guilt I felt for not accomplishing wonderful things in the world. Yes, I do have an interesting career, but I've worked hard to develop it over the past nine years. I've focused on my work, my child, myself, to the exclusion of making a commitment to a man. I could not have done everything at once.

I read all the women's magazines every month; and I pick the areas of *me* I want to perfect. That means I skip the chocolate torte recipes and the little self-improvement pop psychology quizzes. And I don't feel guilty about any of it anymore. That is the ultimate liberation: not feeling guilty for what you are not, what you have not done or accumulated.

An old friend, a forty-one-year-old divorced mother of three who lives in Kansas City, told me over lunch one day, "I have never admitted this to anyone else, but a few years ago when I went back to grad school at night, I almost gave up my kids. I thought they would have to live with their father because I honestly didn't know how I would manage it all, how I would get it all done. I was setting impossible goals for myself, but I didn't know they were impossible. They seemed normal to me, you know?

"So I had this big talk with the kids and I told them we just couldn't manage. I couldn't keep us all together if I added one more thing to my list of obligations. And I had to have the master's degree to get a promotion; and I needed the promotion because we had to have more money.

"Two of the kids refused to leave. My thirteen-year-old daughter sat on my lap. She said I was trying to get rid of them; and we both cried. My older son did go to his father's, but he came back in two weeks. I thought he would be happy there because his father is a prominent surgeon. He has a lot of money.

"Well, we had another talk and this time they told me they had worked everything out. They knew what they would do to help with the housework. They told me things I didn't need to do anymore; and they were right about most of it.

"I still thought it wouldn't work. I was afraid I was going to lose my mind. So I started jogging. And somehow we managed. We made our own rules.

"Their father says we live like gypsies. When they told him I was running, he said I was crazy. He said I couldn't add another thing to what I was already doing. What he didn't understand was I stopped adding when I started running. And I began subtracting— eliminating things I didn't want or need to do like planting tulip bulbs in the fall and baking Christmas cookies and polishing my nails.

"My life became so wonderfully focused: I went to work; I came home and ran; I went to school; and I came home and talked to the kids.

"It only stopped working so well when I met a man and got involved with him. After we broke up, I started running again. And my life started working again. I'm not sure what that says about men, about me. Maybe it just means I don't have time for a man yet until the kids are gone. And if so, well, okay.

"The night we broke up I couldn't sleep. I got out of bed at 2:00 A.M. and decided to run for a few blocks, just to get the stress out. I am not a nut about running. I won't run in the snow or when it's 100 degrees. But I knew I needed to run this night.

"When I started, I was crying and my nose was stuffy so I had to breathe out of my mouth. And I hadn't run in two months because I was so wrapped up in this man. I was puffing like crazy. I only did a mile, a very slow mile. Halfway through, the snot ran down my nose and I wiped it away with my hand and I could breathe again.

"And it didn't hurt so much to run. I knew I was going to be all right, to get back to the place where I had been.

"You know I was never farther from having it all at any time in my life. I had three kids who were rapidly outgrowing me, no man, a so-so job. But I never felt better in my life. I was free. It was more than a runner's high."

I told this story to Jillian, a confirmed nonrunner, and she said, "Oh, yes, I know the feeling. One day I was standing in front of a magazine rack in a supermarket. I decided I wasn't chic enough for *Vogue* and I was too old for *Mademoiselle,* and *House Beautiful* had nothing to say to my apartment. And I had been buying those three magazines forever, usually not reading them, but buying them.

"I thought, taken together, they were what I should be. They always made me feel guilty; and I thought it was because I spent money on them and then didn't read them. That day I knew they made me feel guilty because I didn't live up to them.

"So I debated all the choices on the magazine rack. I read the tables of contents. I finally bought *Family Circle* for some muffin recipes and *Mademoiselle* for a Joyce Carol Oates story, not the image. And I felt free.

"I had finally stopped buying promises—and guilt. I had begun to buy only what I wanted to read. And I felt so grown up then."

Dr. Susie would probably tell these women they were failing "to maximize their potential."

12

Where Are We Going?

> ...*One group is paying a high price for these social changes: women of the feminist generation, the baby boomers, the great glut of talented, beautiful women whom I call—in my more cynical moments—the Desperate Straights.*
> —Amanda Spake in *Ms.* magazine, November 1984

J illian told me she was "no longer desperate" and had decided there was "no man out there" for her on her thirty-seventh birthday. We were drinking a bottle of champagne in some dark restaurant on Illinois 157, one of those places with wood-paneled walls, an enormous stone fireplace, and swords crossed on the walls. She said, "Oh, well. I don't mind anymore. I really don't. The changes ahead will be wrought by a huge group of unmarried women. Married women will never risk too much by pushing too far. I can't wait until a lot of other women decide there's no man out there for them too. We will be the cutting edge."

It was very hot outside, probably 100-plus. I had just come from Lindenwood College, the then summer home of the football Cardinals, where I'd interviewed Charlie Davis, a massive man, about the death of a friend. Davis had cried. My mind was on him and on my lover, Ryan, who had already let himself into my apartment with his key and was waiting for me between cool sheets. Immersed in thoughts of men, I didn't recognize the significance of Jillian's announcement.

We toasted to "the next revolution."

She will be forty-one in a few months; and "the next revolution" has not come. Only the fashions have changed.

But, no matter what the proponents of "traditional values" may

158

tell us, we cannot go back. The feminine mystique is dead. Yet we aren't moving forward either. The feminist mystique hasn't served us well, as well as we'd hoped.

The long-awaited, and frequently announced, second stage of the women's movement reminds me of an old car in sub-zero weather. It grinds, then starts, stops, turns over again, jerks wildly for a while, kicks out. We don't need a new mystique, another myth. What we need is feminist pragmatism, a hard-headed, no-nonsense realism, the kind of reality a mechanic would employ to fix that old car. We do not need another public relations executive who will order a new paint job, another set of publicity stills, and press releases announcing, THE NEW MYSTIQUE, THE SECOND STAGE RE-TURNS.

The numbers will force us to change. Those numbers are not exactly reassuring: The disparity between men and women, the gender-pay gap, the increasing ranks of the female poor. No wonder we want to cover them up with the pancake makeup of imagery. But we have to learn to look at them as Jane Fonda is teaching us to look at the tiny lines in our faces and see hard-won gains, not losses. We have to look at these numbers and see not the privileges they take away from us but the opportunities for growth they pro-vide us.

Exercise buffs—and I am one—swear by the motto "no gain without pain." We have been experiencing the pain. We *can* turn it into real gains.

As Jillian predicted on her thirty-seventh birthday, the heroine for the 1980s may be the happily unmarried woman. No Cinderella or Sleeping Beauty, she will *not* have her happiness bestowed upon her by the love of a male. No cinematic heroine like Jill Clayburgh, she will have outgrown the initial heady but insecure stage of being alone. And unlike Dr. Susie, she won't be required to earn her happiness by extraordinary performance on all fronts. Experience will set as well on her as those fragile lines on Fonda's face.

Our heroine will be a real person, an ordinary woman who has achieved happiness the old-fashioned way, by making adult choices and living by them. A woman of quiet honor, she will be a prag-matist, who doesn't let her tight grip on reality diminish her joie de vivre. Definitely, she will not live her life in the expectation that marriage someday will change it.

Though we are faced with shrinking options, few of us have admitted our lives are not full of the same possibilities, the same choices we had, or thought we had, a decade ago. We still think the choices have to do largely with men, with pleasing them. And we still ask, "What can I do to make the relationship work, to get this man to marry me?" more often than we ask, "What is this relationship doing for me?" We must learn that most of our choices have nothing to do with men, with marriage. They are *our* choices to make, *our* lives to shape.

To date, we've not chosen to make real women our role models. We still hang on the words of the rich and famous celebrity, the $100,000-a-year woman. This week, rock singer Pat Benatar, eight months pregnant, told yet another interviewer, "You can have it all," as she described her plans for taking baby on rock tours—and yet another interviewer presented her maternity with reverence and quoted her as if she really were some kind of example for us.

Most of us will never take babies on rock tours, graduate from law school, raise six kids, and win the Pillsbury Bake-Off all at once. Yet we have no one else to emulate but the women who do. They and men have told us what happiness is and where we can find it; and we have believed them and gone questing for it.

"I don't think any woman *can* be happy until she writes her own definition of happy," Jillian says. "Women have always been too ready to accept other people's definitions, to assume there is no happiness unless it is, at least in part, *man*-made."

Never has that been a more dangerous assumption than it is today.

There are simply not enough men to go around and some of us will never marry, some will never mother unless they do so alone. Others have waited too long for Mr. Right and their fertility has ebbed away. The basic contract we have always made with men—protection in exchange for acceptance of male authority—has never been more tenuous than it is today.

As long as our safety, security, happiness, depends on men, we are doomed to be unsafe, insecure, unhappy.

Most women will be single for some considerable period during their adult lives. The overwhelming majority of women will have to work for most of their lives. The statistics make it clear: We no longer have the traditional female options—full-time housewife, part-time low-wage worker. They are disappearing from our lives the way oversize cars disappeared from our highways in the 1970s. The totally dependent wife is an endangered species.

We really cannot retreat to our wombs and homes again. Are women ready to acknowledge this? Can we admit some choices no longer exist? If we can, we will begin to discover other choices we never knew we had.

Do single women have a life plan that does not include marriage? If we do, we are truly free to choose our own paths. If we don't, we are trapped in the underbrush of mythology.

Can we be happy alone? Because where we are going, at least 8 million of us are going there alone. It all comes down to that.

"Some of us are never going to get married or remarried," Colleen says. "And of this group who won't marry, some won't mind at all. I know women who don't want marriage, who have strong career drives, or deep needs for independence. They don't trust men.

"The rest of us would like to marry. We are getting increasingly nervous as we pass thirty and feel the biological time clock ticking down. We have to make some decisions fast; and we know it. If we don't eventually marry, some of us will be disappointed, but I don't think *devastated*. We will survive. We are used to being alone; and we are survivors.

"The women I know who no longer have the expectation—or in many cases, the desire—of marriage are the happiest. They may have made themselves unhappy as long as they still expected to get married someday. When they gave it up, the expectation that is, they were happier. That doesn't mean they won't marry if they find someone, but they are no longer counting on finding someone.

"Those of us who still want to get married carry this desire around with us all the time. If we're in a dead-end relationship, we wonder if we should get out and look for one that will lead to marriage or if we should hang in there and hope he'll change. If we're in no relationship at all we panic because we're losing time. Either way, the lack of progress toward our goals nags at us constantly.

"The worst is not knowing for sure if you're on the right track or not, if this is a dead-end relationship or one that will develop, given time and patience. I've been involved with Ken for more than four years. I ask myself how much longer I'm going to give this. It's comfortable. It works on a day-to-day basis. Certainly it's preferable to being alone. But is it going anywhere?

"So often in the past six months I have wondered if I am wasting my time and cutting myself off from meeting a man who might share my goals and want the same things I want, marriage and kids.

"The longer we're together the more skeptical I get. It's hard to believe he'll ever change. Then I tell myself, 'Well, if I'm not going to get married at all, I guess this is the kind of relationship I would like to have.'

"One part of me really wants marriage. The other part says, 'If you don't get married you'll make it. You've been taking care of yourself since you were eighteen. You can keep doing it. You're doing just fine.'

"I know I can do it. I used to think I could never stand to be alone in my thirties. Now I think that will be okay; and I can look into my forties and see myself alone and believe that will be okay too. Probably when it gets closer, I will feel the same way about being alone in my fifties.

"I really am one of those women who can manage alone if I have to do that. Not just manage, I could make a life for myself that is happy."

Although Colleen wants marriage, she is planning her life now as if it will never happen. She and Anne have obtained financial backing and will be opening their own public relations firm within months.

"You can't make any money working for someone else," she says. "I want more money than I'm making now. I am tired of being underpaid. I know Allen's going to be disappointed in me—and Jessica will be angry for a while. Last year I would have stayed put rather than hurt and anger them. But I can't let personal feelings influence business decisions. I've done that before; and I won't do it again.

"I am taking my life into my own hands.

"I haven't told anyone, but I stopped taking the birth control pill a year ago. Didn't you guess when we talked at Power's bar that night and I said I wondered what Ken would do if I got pregnant?

"We don't have sex often enough to justify the use of the pill. Well, I want a child; and I wouldn't mind if I got pregnant, so I stopped taking it. But he doesn't know I've stopped. If I do get pregnant, it will force the issue of marriage between us. If he wants to break up, I am not going to force him to pay child support. After all, I am doing this behind his back. It is a little selfish, underhanded certainly.

"But he is selfish too, very much so.

"If we're going to break up, I'd rather we split over something very serious, something important, rather than a minor disagreement. Maybe deep down he needs this to push him into marriage. Maybe he wants it to happen. I don't really think so. I won't pursue him if he doesn't want me, but I want the baby.

"If I get pregnant, I will probably resort to subterfuge and tell him the pill failed. I'll tell him if he doesn't want to become more involved, I understand.

"My doctor suggested fertility tests if I am not pregnant in the next few months. I will take them. I would rather discover a problem now and try to treat it while there's time. Wouldn't it be awful to learn after thirty-five, as so many women have, that you're not fertile and you're too old to adopt?

"I'd rather have a father for my child and a good marriage for myself, but a strong second choice for me is having a child alone. And I want the father to be someone I love. I wouldn't want to tell my child, 'Your father was someone I hardly knew.' I would want my child to know he was conceived in love.

"I don't want to miss the experience of motherhood. I'll probably only have one child, but I do want this one child."

Whatever you may think of her approach, Colleen isn't *waiting* for marriage to provide her with the opportunity for motherhood or the economic life-style she wants. She has decided *she* will choose to mother. *She* will control her standard of living. Maybe the choice of marriage will be denied her, but she recognizes other options do exist.

Jillian says, "I don't think women my age understood that there were choices beyond the obvious: You got married or you didn't. Whichever choice you made, married or single, determined the rest of your life: whether you would have a child or not, whether you would have much money or not, where you would live, *everything*."

Women got one choice; all the other choices hinged on a man. Today it is different. The one choice we may no longer have is whether or not to marry.

But we do have all the others.

Most of us really did not mean to be single forever when we chose the single life a decade ago. But some of us did, especially formerly marrieds. Jenny *meant* to be alone today when she divorced her husband ten years ago.

A petite woman who doesn't color her short gray hair, Jenny is fifty-five and the mother of four children in their twenties.

"Getting a divorce at forty-five was a scary thing to do," she says. "I was raised Catholic. And women my age, especially Catholic women, did not get divorced. But it was also an exhilarating thing to do.

"When people tell me they admire my courage for leaving, I tell them staying married really takes more courage. I took the easy way out.

"And I did it because I wanted the control of my life I'd never had.

"Marriage had its delightful aspects, especially financial security. I was married to a man who owned a successful business. He was generous; and I had everything I wanted. But when I was miserable, I was *so* miserable. It's easier to get out of an unhappy marriage, to do things by yourself, than to stay and be miserable.

"I can't stand anger; and I was married to an angry man. He would go out of town on Monday mad about some minor thing and come home Friday night still mad about the same little thing, which is ridiculous to me. And he was always changing the ground rules. I never knew where I stood.

"I couldn't live with that—with having my life so controlled by someone who operated on a completely arbitrary set of rules.

"A lot of divorced women like to talk about what they find most pleasant about being single, which is usually the freedom—freedom from a regular schedule of meals, visiting someone else's relatives, buying someone else's food, clothes, headache pills. What I like is the control. For the first time in my life I am in control of everything. I make the decisions. I'm not just talking about the simple things, like not cooking if I don't want to cook.

"That's a small part of it. I am in control of everything. I don't think of myself as an extremely religious person, but I am somewhat religious, even though I have affairs with married men, which would horrify my family. Well, now I am in control of whether I am Catholic or not, of how Catholic I am. No one else judges me on that. I can just lie to my mother; and I do. I can lie to my mother with the best of them.

"My four brothers and I were raised by my mother and grand-father. My father died when I was ten. Grandfather was the dominant figure in my life. He lived with my aunt, who had never married. She was a very strong, impressive woman. No one ever won my grandfather's approval—or my mother's for that matter.

"Grandfather paid our way. He bought us a home, our food, clothing, gave us our allowances, sent us to college. He ruled my mother and he ruled us. His standards were very high. He came to visit every Sunday afternoon and had meetings with us about money. He asked what we had charged at the department stores that week, what we needed in the week ahead. We had a very strict accounting.

"He was generous, but he was in charge, like my husband was in charge during our marriage. You know I am still attracted to powerful men. I had a long affair with a married man, very wealthy, who was powerful, strong like my grandfather. He would take me on trips and give me money for shopping; and I saved the money to pay the bills. If he caught me, he would get mad and say, 'I'll give you the money you need for your bills, just ask. This money is for you to blow, to have fun.' But I couldn't do it.

"Eventually we broke up because I felt guilty about his wife. I was in love with him, but I never really wanted to marry him. I am attracted to power, but I don't want to live under it again. If I ever do marry again, it will be for economic security in my old age—or because I am so crazy about a man I can't bear to share him with anyone else *and* I think marriage would hold him.

"I would not marry again to please a man. When I finally realized I could never please my husband no matter what I did—any more than I could ever please my mother or my grandfather—I was free. Now I only have to please myself."

We didn't read about women like Jenny, a happily unmarried woman, ten years ago when feminist heroines were in vogue because she didn't walk out on her children, she didn't go back to graduate school, she didn't become an entrepreneur and earn a lot of money. As an administrative assistant to an architect in Indiana, she earns $15,000 a year. Hers isn't a glamorous or dramatic story. It is remarkably free of trauma. Her children love her. She has become friends with her ex-husband since the divorce.

"We are capable of intimacy now; we weren't when we were married. I'm sure our closeness is because of the children. We will always share them. Somehow it's easier to admit your children have faults to their father than it is to admit this to anyone else. He is good to them; and I have no anger toward him.

"I paid my dues; and I have a nice life, a very satisfactory life now."

After I talked to Jenny, I wondered what makes a "nice life" for a single woman. Sheron believes money is the key—but Jenny is happy on a modest income. Formerly married women often tell me they are happier than never married women because they know what marriage is really like—and because they usually have children who keep them from feeling lonely, unconnected to the world. But Jillian is happy; and she has never been married, has never mothered.

Is there a common denominator between happily unmarried women?

Jenny is pretty, bright, witty, and fun. The description also applies to some unhappily single women. She has close family ties, a support network of friends and business associates, interests and hobbies, and lovers. So do the unhappy ones. Those are the things the magazines tell us we need in order to live happily alone.

Jenny says, "They are not enough. We need something else, something deeper, something inside us. Self-esteem is more important than anything else in determining if you can be happy alone or not.

"Several years ago my daughter taught me that. She was rattling pans and rustling around the kitchen preparing a casserole only she would eat. I went in and asked her why she bothered to go to all that trouble for one meal, why she didn't just fix a sandwich.

"And she said, 'Mother, I'm good enough to cook for.'

"I knew then she had self-esteem; and she would always be okay. She is a beautifully secure girl; and I will never worry about her happiness because she is.

"I have self-esteem too. I like being alone because I am good company. I may not bother to cook meals for myself very often because I don't like to cook that much—I had enough of cooking—but I make time for myself. I do the things I enjoy, watching old movies on public television, reading, manicuring my nails. I love to read.

"I am very happy when I am alone reading a book."

Jillian also has self-esteem.

Another friend who had gone through a painful, unwanted divorce a few years ago said she wished she could live as happily alone as Jillian did—but she couldn't because "Jillian thinks well of herself." She added, "I need someone else around, someone to get out of bed for each day other than me."

Jillian says, "I am worth making a life for. I don't think self-esteem is connected necessarily to income. I wish I earned more money, but my income doesn't affect how I feel about myself."

Kara, on the other hand, identifies money as the one element missing from her life, the one element that keeps her from being "totally happy single."

"It's hard to have self-respect when you don't have money," she says. "In our society money is still the measure of personal worth. I don't feel as good about myself as I would like to feel. You know how I react when a man begins to like me too much; I think there must be something wrong with him, because deep down I don't like me that much.

"I'm sure it all goes back to my relationship with my father. I could never win his love and approval, though I tried hard. He always favored my brother. Now he is doing the same things with my stepsister and stepbrother as he did with us. Boys are first. They count more than girls. It's an all-pervasive attitude in our culture. He certainly isn't the only one. I don't think things will change a great deal in our society until this attitude has changed. It's hard for women to make their own life plans when they've grown up thinking they're not the same as, not as good as, a man."

Maybe this reasoning is why Kara doesn't make life plans.

People who know her are surprised she has remained in a government job when she has so much intelligence, creativity, energy.

"She is one of the brightest people I have ever met," a friend once said. "Why the hell doesn't she get someone to back her in a business of her own?"

I'm never sure how to respond to such comments. She *is* bright; she *could* successfully manage a business, handle any career she wanted to have. Jillian, who is also bright, is content with a "mere job."

She says, "I get tired of people asking me why I'm not accomplishing more. If I had a profession, I wouldn't have the time to do everything else I like doing. A balanced life is important to me. I'm not a workaholic. Time is more important to me than money. I've never known anyone who had both time and money at once—except the independently wealthy.

"I have chosen this. Some women don't develop their work lives fully because they are waiting for a man to rescue them, because they don't feel good enough, or because they sublimate their goals to a husband's. Those women haven't chosen; they have let someone else choose for them."

If we ask why Kara and Jillian aren't accomplishing "more," are we not imposing the Superwoman standard again by indicting women who choose not to be overachievers? Is there really something wrong with holding an ordinary job?

Lynne says she feels the "push to achieve" very strongly.

"Educated single women my age and younger are driven internally and externally. An ordinary job isn't acceptable. The only way out of the big career trap is to be creative and funky. You can be poor and even lazy if you run a vintage clothing shop or sell antiques. People will find you eccentric, charming—especially if you also know where to find good cheap wine and know some interesting, powerful people.

"I do think the pressure to achieve has made women look at marriage as a haven again. It's so intense. Marriage looks good, a reason to back off, let down a little. Even if you still have to work, you have an excuse for not doing quite as much as you did before.

"We are the first generation of women to experience this pressure. The battle between the independent woman and the dependent one goes on inside most of us at least part of the time. I know this relationship with Roger isn't working for me. He is getting much more out of it than I am. I can't depend on him to show up when he says he will. His work, his political campaign, always take precedence over me. He seldom takes me out; and he doesn't even bring a bottle of wine over when he has dinner here.

"He's owed me $25 for four weeks. When I asked him for it, he said, 'That just proves a man should never borrow money from a woman.' He pulled out his wallet, threw four dollars at me, and said that's all he had.

"My friends ask me what I am doing with him; and I honestly don't know. Well, I know. The dependent woman sniffs a male, a potential rescuer—even though he obviously isn't reliable. I'm kidding myself; and I know it, but I do it.

"I work the phones for his campaign. I support him in every way. What am I getting out of it? I can say I have a man—for what that's worth.

"He called me at the last minute on Saturday night to do a movie.

I had tickets to the symphony with friends. After the symphony, we stopped at Culpepper's for a drink. As we walked in, he was leaving with three sleazy girls, hairdresser types in cheap rabbit coats. They were going dancing.

"He said he would come back in an hour and join me and my friends. He didn't. Over two hours later I left Culpepper's and waited by his car. We had a big fight. He accused me of acting like the wronged wife; he said I had embarrassed him and set the relationship back. He said, 'We can't be friends if there is no trust.'

"The next night he called and invited me over for a steak dinner. I tried to explain my side: He had embarrassed me in front of my friends; he shouldn't have said he was going to join us and then not shown up; I wasn't spying.

"Then we had another one of those talks where I tried to tell him he doesn't give me anything in the relationship. He keeps saying he can't help it that he's busy. He asks me if I think he enjoys working so hard and never having time for fun. He asks me to understand, be patient.

"Then he asks me if I'll be able to finish all those campaign phone calls.

"But after we had dinner together, I told myself that he needs me. I believed I was really the one calling the shots in the relationship, that his feelings had just been hurt because I wouldn't change my plans to be with him.

"For the next week, I tried to pin him down to a night we could get together before he went to Colorado to take his boys skiing and I went to Florida with friends. He finally said Friday night. I changed plans to be available. He didn't show up. I tracked him down at the office; and he said he would be late. I finally went out around eleven. When I came home at one, there was a message on the machine: 'Honey, I'm home now. Sorry I'm late. Call me.'

"He doesn't ask me to do anything unless it means helping him. I'm with him, but he doesn't see me. He doesn't know who I am at all. I could be any woman. I have the privilege of going over there late at night when he's through with other things, when he is ready to sleep.

"What am I getting out of this? He's happier in this relationship than I am. Why do women hang on to men like this simply so we won't be alone?

"Last summer when I wasn't involved with a man at all I was

so happy. I read books. And I can tell I'm not happy now because I haven't read a book for the last three months. I have to feel calm, settled, relaxed in my life before I read. And I miss reading. Last summer I also discovered pottery.

"And I was so happy! I should get back to that feeling. Why do we forget how happy we can be without men? Why do we forget everything, especially our pride, when we get involved with them?"

Lynne went to a psychic before Christmas; and the psychic predicted a marriage proposal this year—exactly what she wanted to hear. For the $40 fee, the psychic also predicted "a trip in the winter with a man."

"Well, she was close to right," Lynne laughs. "He's taking a trip; and so am I. We're just not taking a trip together. I wish he would have asked me to take a trip with him."

Lynne vacillates between believing in psychics and science—between the warring needs of the dependent and independent woman inside her.

"I made a New Year's resolution this year to get married," she says. "I want to get married this year; and I thought it would be Roger. Maybe it won't. Maybe he can't change; and I certainly can't stand the way he is. I'm not the kind of woman who can adapt to his kind of life. I want more attention.

"Maybe I was just taken in at the beginning. Power, status, a good line—haven't they always taken women in?

"I want to get married very much, but if I don't get married, I do have a plan. I am still buying fifties furniture; and I will get a ranch house in an older subdivision. I can afford that alone. The experience of birth doesn't mean a lot to me. And I'm afraid of raising a little baby all alone.

"There are older children, biracial children, nobody wants to adopt. I could adopt a child who needs a lot of love, because I have a lot of love to give. I think I would be happy, satisfied in my own home with a child. And I know I would be a good mother.

"I would rather be single than settle for disaster. Roger is beginning to look like disaster. Besides, he hasn't mentioned marriage. I don't know if he even thinks about me that way."

For Lynne, the conclusion—"I'd rather be single than settle for disaster"—represents years of therapy. She has been steadily groping toward a state of mind that reflects independence, self-esteem. And she knows she isn't there yet.

"My therapist told me to look in the mirror every morning and say to myself, 'You are a terrific person, a wonderful woman.' I am beginning to believe it.

"If Roger calls, I will probably give in to him again. I will believe what he says and not what he does. And of course he doesn't believe me when I tell him he is going to lose me because I always come back. He believes what I do, not what I say."

Women do believe what men say and choose to ignore their actions when the actions don't match their soothing words. Roger stands Lynne up; he says he loves her. She believes in his words. Men ignore our rhetoric and pick up on our behavior. We spout independence, freedom, liberation—but we come when they call, we expect them to pick up the check. Of course they believe in the feminine behavior, not the feminist words.

Christine, a New Yorker and editor of a women's publication, is in her early thirties. She says, "The basic problem is that women are not used to independence yet. Men pick up on our insecurity, make note of all our unsure moves. In spite of our rhetoric, we are still not weaned from dependence on men. We don't have the deep sense of self-confidence, the pride in achievement men have.

"It's crazy that in the 1980s everyone would be so uptight about being single. Even in New York City, where there is a big percentage of single people and a thriving singles life-style, all my friends seem to be getting married or having babies. When you see everyone around you pairing off and nesting, you feel less secure about what you are doing—especially if you are a first-generation feminist leading a life women have not led before.

"In the 1970s everyone was single; and there was security in numbers. Now the position of being single seems shaky."

Christine has been divorced for ten years. The brief and unmemorable union produced no children, no hard feelings, no lingering friendship. She has spent the past decade building a career, first in television, then journalism. She is a good editor, very effective in part because she is such a conscientious career builder. When she assumes control of a publication, she works hard to make it a product that will showcase *her* abilities.

"Being good at your job is important if you're going to be happily single," she says. "Some women have gotten discouraged with their career progress or been daunted by the challenges—and let those feelings convince them they are unhappy about being single.

"As women get better at their jobs and more comfortable in being assertive on the job, they will be more comfortable with being single.

"Giving and taking criticism has been hard for working women. Asking more money—a fair starting salary, a deserved raise—is also hard. Women until very recently have had little experience at being anything but nice. Society has always rewarded nice women. Most of us were still raised to be nice.

"If you're going to get somewhere professionally, you have to stop being nice, to stop worrying about the amenities, about being well behaved.

"I think women are learning to speak up professionally, especially those who have been in the workplace for a decade or more.

"Gradually the job assertiveness will change our personal lives too. The hope is: If we learn to ask for what we deserve at work, we will be able to do this in our relationships with men."

Lynne, who no longer has trouble collecting overdue accounts, raising her fees, or soliciting work, is beginning to use her assertiveness skills with men. "At least I know now when I am letting myself be used as a chump. I let men get away with things I wouldn't let my women friends get away with—like owing me money.

"I know men treat me better at the beginning of a relationship. Is that because familiarity really does breed contempt? Or is it because I will do less for men in the beginning and appear to value myself more? I expect more from them at first. I tell ι. γ. elf I am terrific; and they are lucky to be with me.

"When I was first seeing Roger, he told me all the time how beautiful and wonderful and high-spirited I was.

"Now I have to ask for compliments, which makes me anxious."

Christine, a svelte blonde who has been on the New York social circuit for eight years, says, "Anxiety is a real turn-off to men. If you're happy and productive and involved in your own life you're appealing. There is no way to fake this state of mind either. You cannot pretend to be all these things to capture a man. If you're not really happy alone, you come off desperate.

"I do believe the few desirable men out there are attracted to the women who aren't absolutely desperate to get them.

"I think I am ready to marry again, though I wasn't ready until now. If I meet someone I want to marry, fine. But I know there is no perfect man, no perfect existence. Being married or being single takes work. I tell people my midlife crisis will probably be to get married and have a baby at forty. My sister got divorced and dyed her hair blond. Whatever it is you didn't do, whatever it is you don't have, begins to look good at forty.

"As I said, I am ready for marriage. I could do it. But my life plans certainly don't revolve around the *possibility*. And I am still having a lot of fun being single.

"A good sense of humor is a single woman's most important asset—for herself I mean, not to make herself appealing to a man. Life is so much more enjoyable if you can laugh. You need to remember everybody goes through the same things and not take your experience so seriously. I have a lot of single women friends; and we indulge in black humor. We even joke about sexual frustration. We ask each other if it was another night with Mr. Plastic Bachelor.

"If we have horrible dates, we share the horror stories and laugh at them. They aren't catastrophes. I had one of those dates recently; and the only good thing about it was I kept thinking all evening, Wait until my friends hear about this one.

"I had forgotten to ask him what he does for a living, a very important question really. Everyone in New York is so career oriented and spends twelve hours a day at the office—so work is the biggest topic of dating conversations. Well, we spent the whole evening driving around Wall Street looking at all the buildings he supplies with toilet paper. If I'd known in advance he's a toilet-paper supplier, I wouldn't have gone out with him.

"You can only laugh about a night like that."

Christine and her friends, all professional women, are fairly critical of the men they meet. In the Midwest we lament the men are all married or gay or nerds. In New York, Christine says, "They are gay, married, neurotic, or workaholics, or several of the above. Sensitive men often turn out to be wimps. A friend says, 'It's not the men who eat quiche you have to watch, but the men who cook it.'

"A lot of New York men are really hyper. So what if there's a rat in the kitchen? Have another drink. Sometimes men forget this is New York, one of the most exciting cities in the world. They spend so much time working out or cooking, they miss everything."

She admits she and her friends are so "picky" about men, they are in danger of becoming terminally single women. "I'd rather be terminally single, having a good time, than miserably married. If anything, I think I will get more picky as the years go by, not less. Some of my friends think there are so many gay men in New York because they are intimidated by modern women. Maybe we are intimidating, but I don't think that's bad.

"Women should not see men as rescuers, knights who can come along and change their lives. We should be selective. We should realize we already have wonderful lives. If a man is going to be an addition to that life, he must have a lot to offer."

Increasingly, single women, even those who want to get married, will adopt this attitude—and resolve *not* to live their lives in the expectation that marriage will change them.

"Happily unmarried women probably know a lot of unhappily married women," Jillian says, "which is a plus. When you see how miserable marriage can be, you are less likely to romanticize it. And really I think the worst thing about marriage is the way women *have* romanticized it. If we were more realistic about marriage, we would see it's not moonlight, magic, and roses, but commitment, work, concentrated energy—admirable qualities all, though not desirable for everyone."

Can we stop romanticizing marriage?

"It's amazing how women project," Christine says. "One date and they are building romantic fantasies, planning marriage with a guy they don't know at all. It does make you wonder. In spite of the women's movement, the gains made, the distance traveled—are we still so desperate for marriage? And why?"

Jenny says, "Marriage is an economic contract; and I think women know this. But I also think they need the illusion of romance as the excuse for the contract.

"I do believe in romance. It has its place in our lives, but marriage is seldom the place. I like married lovers because they are so romantic. They know all they can give you is tenderness in bed, a flower, maybe a small gift, romance—because at home they are paying the bills and participating in perfunctory sex. Married lovers are romantic as long as you aren't married to them.

"But all of life isn't supposed to be a romance novel. Women who do not excessively romanticize men and especially marriage have more fun. I have a group of women friends who meet once a month for drinks. We call ourselves the International Crotch Watchers Society because we like to look and we aren't looking at chins. Women can be wonderfully raunchy about sex. We are fun when we're being raunchy. How much fun have you ever had with someone who is dripping dew?"

Odds are the woman who is "dripping dew" is primarily committed to marriage because of its economic advantages—a fact she would never, could ever, articulate through the rose bud clenched in her teeth. The *very* traditional woman is a predator in lip gloss, a fact not lost on some men, especially those under thirty-five.

"Once you have made your peace with being single," Jillian says, "and stopped being desperate, you stop acting like a predator. At that point, you can make your peace with men and start enjoying them as human beings, not as potential saviors, wage earners, not as the purchasers of insurance policies that will list you as the beneficiary."

These women have close ties with men as brothers, fathers, sons, friends, lovers—if not as husbands. "Such close ties," Jillian says, "are a benefit of being single."

Jenny says, "My brother is my best friend." She also has a steady man who plays a role in her life not unlike the role Ned plays for Kara: something more than a friend, yet not a love. Kara always has several men in her life who provide a balance between lovers, friends, work associates. Single women's lives are not devoid of men, not lacking in male companionship because we are not married.

In fact, we probably have more men in our lives than married women do.

Jillian says, "It's much easier for an unmarried woman to have close male friends than for a married woman. Marriage seems very limiting to me. You are not supposed to want or need anything else from any other man than your husband. Maybe this is changing somewhat, but not fast. The women I know who have husbands are still constrained by their relationships with them."

Certainly I know men better now than I ever did as a wife. I look at them and see something other than a paycheck stub. I only really get angry at them if they look without seeing *someone,* a person. And the last thing I want from them is promises one or both of us won't keep.

The last thing any of us need anymore is the insidious promise of protection in exchange for acceptance of male authority.

The agreement may have worked well, once upon a time, when somebody had to fend off the saber-toothed tiger because we were too pregnant to waddle. And we were pregnant most of the time until we died in childbirth. The agreement doesn't work anymore.

Kara says, "Men still use it to stay in power. Violence is always implicit in male-female relationships. If we get too much power, they could always beat us up and take it back. And I think they would."

The women's movement is never going to shift into high gear until we admit the agreement doesn't work anymore, the promise is no longer being kept. Women have loved men and marriage too much and ourselves not enough. We have worked for the love of work for too long now. It's time to work for financial reward. We have allowed romance too much room in our lives—to the exclusion of pragmatism. And we have bought into every myth consistently presented to us in slick magazines.

Where are we going?

If we let the statistics roll over us like tidal waves, women are going to the poorhouse, along with their children, in record numbers. Until we stop regarding marriage as the economic solution of choice, we will not achieve pay equality. But if we can begin to look at marriage the way men look at it, we will stop being *desperate* to be married—and start demanding from men, business, government, society, the changes we need to become truly independent. We may marry or not, but we don't need to be married to care adequately for our children and ourselves.

This wasn't supposed to happen. Eight million women were not supposed to end up alone with the choice to marry or not taken away from us. We weren't supposed to be standing here with empty dance cards in our hands—but we are. It has happened.

What are we going to make of it? Do we stand desperately on the sidelines wringing our hands—or invent new steps those dancing in pairs will envy?

13

And How Are We Going to Get There?

American women are not only the only people in the world who manage to lose track of themselves, but we do seem to mislay the past in a singularly absent-minded fashion.
—"Reflections on the History of Women" by Elizabeth Janeway, from *Women: Their Changing Roles* (1973)

Feminism: the principle that women should have political, economic, and social rights equal to those of men.
                    —*Webster's New World Dictionary*

Rob has a sign over his desk, bold black letters on glossy white. It says, SEX AND MONEY.

Think about those words: *sex* and *money*. They are governed by laws, religious and civil, yet they encompass the most intimate details of our lives. Sex and money. Are they the solutions or the problems? According to Rob, "Both."

Certainly single women have been defining our problems in sex-and-money terms.

Women have created a romantic belief system around the sex drive. The sexual revolution notwithstanding, few women accept lust as *lust*. We prefer to equate the wet vagina with love. And love is romanticized, enshrined in marriage.

We live in the 1980s, yet women tell me they never have sex without love, they don't masturbate. (Or they'd rather not talk about it if they do.) Women act as if masturbation were a lurid detail in male fantasies. I have two married friends who swear they have never masturbated; and I believe them. I believe they would never take that kind of control of their own bodies, would never grant themselves solitary sexual pleasure not connected with "love." Well, I am not in love with my lover; and I do masturbate. And I am sorry these women do not know the joys of sex based on lust. I am sorry they have never discovered that self-stimulation is just fun.

Inveterate romantic junkies that women are, we have been almost as romantic about money as we have been about sex. We have married money and lusted after it. Artists fear it, yuppies worship it, and women treat it like the hot potato—spend it before it burns us. Very few of us have been practical about getting our fair share.

We still have an inordinate amount of trouble asking for what is ours. "We need years of practice to do what men do naturally," Christine says: "walk into the boss's office and ask for a raise."

Recently I told my male business-writing partner he had not carried his weight on a project; and because he had not, I would not split the fee evenly. In the past I would have worried about risking our friendship by speaking up. I would have kept quiet, divided the fee evenly, and resented him. Or I would have tried to speak and cried. (And he would have blamed the tears on my hormones.) So strong is the power of female conditioning, it's only taken me nine years of being single and self-employed to reach this point—the point Christine describes as "acting on the knowledge you're not a little girl sheltered by your parents anymore."

The majority of us go to work every day in female-dominated occupations where we are not paid commensurate with men who have the same level of skills, education, training experience—but work in male-dominated occupations. Or we work side by side with management men performing the same jobs—and earning less money. We accept these conditions as normal, like snow in winter. Our child-support checks don't come in the mail; and we consider that a part of being female, like having a period.

We think that men are part of the problem; and we believe they could be, will be, the solution.

If we applied feminist pragmatism to sex and money, we could turn them into the solutions, not the problems. We can't solve the problems of being a woman alone by getting married. A husband can't get us equal or comparable pay in the work force. A second husband may increase your household income, but he won't redress the child-support grievances you have against the first husband. And there is no such thing as finding a new daddy for the kids.

I am a happily unmarried woman, in control of my sex life, beginning to understand at least how to control my finances. And I owe my happiness in large measure to joint custody. I believe in fathers. That so many divorced women assume fatherhood ends or is greatly diminished by divorce bothers me. We don't expect divorce to end our motherhood do we?

Shared custody is a pragmatic custodial arrangement, respectful of the rights of both parents and child. Sharing custody establishes a better standard of living for the child than he would probably have on his mother's income alone and saves one custodial parent the loneliness and exhaustion inherent in single parenthood. It is a viable alternative to the feminization of poverty.

Looking at my life, I can analyze happiness and attribute it to a lot of little choices about sex and money. I have almost forgotten the time when every little personal choice I made had a political connotation. Apparently, we have all almost forgotten that time.

Kara and I have been talking a lot lately about where we are going and how we are going to get there: "we" meaning she and I, "we" meaning women in general. We keep trying to define a course of action. Will it be personal, political, a blend of the two approaches?

She would like to save money, maybe move or take a trip, or find the motivation to go back to school, look for another job.

And I am at a crossroads: My son is nearly out of high school. For the first time in twenty years, I can live where I want to live. And where is that? Do I want to pursue public relations to the exclusion of journalism, or vice versa? My career is also at a cross-roads. Where am I going and how am I going to get there? Where are women going—and does that have anything to do with me, with Kara?

"I just drift," Kara says, "with no real plan, and I know it. I don't like it. Women in general seem to be drifting now, waiting for things to change. I'm not happy about how I manage or rather don't manage my money. I'm broke too often.

"Around Christmas I really resented Curt because he never takes me out. He always comes over here. I began to resent that so much, more than usual, because I was broke. I told him he would have to start paying something for sex because he contributed nothing to me in any other way. I was half joking and half not. He did pay a few times. Then right after Christmas he gave me $50 to help with the groceries. I felt like he owed it to me, you know? He'd spend that much taking me out to dinner one night.

"I should make a budget, I hate budgets."

I hate budgets too. Kara and I chastise ourselves about not applying feminist pragmatism to our finances as we do our sex lives. We find it easier to talk in sweeping terms about economic progress for women than to develop our own independent financial plans. And maybe that is part of the problem we label the "money problem." Neither of us has been "political" in a while, but increasingly we feel economic answers for women will be found in organization, through politics. But millions of women may have to wrestle with their budgets and their delinquent child-support payments for a while longer before they make the mental leap from the personal to the political.

Other women, however, disagree with Kara and me. They think women must and will all find their personal answers to economic problems. These women are alienated—and not without good cause—from the political process.

Colleen insists, "Feminism is dead or at least not viable today. The ground swell just died out. I don't know any woman, personally or professionally, who considers herself a feminist. Women are working individually to get what they want. They are playing hardball; and they are playing the game alone."

Christine says, "None of my friends calls herself a feminist either. That's passé. I've done that; I've been there. I was the first woman reporter at a TV station. I did the whole number.

"Women are concerned about workplace issues now. We have switched from reading *Ms.* to *Working Woman* and *Savvy.* Nobody talks about Steinem or Friedan. There are other issues.

"Women are fighting for themselves rather than for a cause. I do think women are supportive of each other. We network naturally rather than in organizations, as we did in the 1970s. We all believe in equal pay for equal work—but feminism, no."

All across the country, women are careful to separate themselves from a women's cause, a feminist movement. They are moving toward their own goals, *personal* goals, alone, they say. Everyone is working for herself.

Can we possibly get where we are going without some kind of organization, specifically without the women's movement behind us? Can we get there without once again synthesizing the personal and the political, maybe this time adjusting the mix of the two in a different way? Interestingly, Sheron, the one woman in this book who does earn $100,000, says no.

"The higher up you go in business the more you understand how sexism works. There's a progression: New management women start out as liberal Democrats, work their way up the ladder and become Republicans by middle management, then become liberal Democrats again *if* they reach the top. The view from the top, if you're a woman, is appalling. So few women make it. So few of the rules have really changed.

"I don't think women want to understand that right now. They are apolitical because of their personal lives. They want to get married, have babies; and they are worried about intimidating men. Successful women do intimidate men. So these women are doing everything they can to hang on to what they've made in their professions while wearing softer clothes and trying to behave like "real women" away from the office. Ten years ago they didn't care about the soft clothes, because they didn't want to marry.

"But there is some carry-over in this 'real woman' behavior from after hours to the office. The softness shows up."

Christine disagrees. "There is no carry-over effect.

"I do think the biggest problem women have with men now is trying not to intimidate them. Men are very confused about how to deal with us. They have become shy. Yes, we do try to be more feminine after hours, but I don't think this affects our attitudes in our jobs. We are still competitive in our careers. It's because we have become so competitive that we are less interested in organized movements perhaps.

"My friend Kay and I spent thirty minutes the other day discussing what we would wear on dates with new men. And we laughed about doing this. We're secure enough to do this now. We don't feel like we have to be this tough woman away from the job like we once felt. I saw Leona Helmsley on '60 Minutes' last week. She has the reputation of being a very tough businesswoman; and she projected that on television. But when her husband is around, she turns very soft, feminine.

"The one reason, a simple reason, women don't speak up at work is they don't know how. They need courses in how to ask for money, promotions, equal treatment. Those things must be accomplished on an individual level. No group can do it for you. It's like being born and dying: You're in it alone when you have to ask a superior for a raise."

Sheron says, "Most women work at jobs where the possibility of a raise beyond a fixed percentage point once or twice a year doesn't even exist. They need the kind of help group action could give them. They need the reinforcement of numbers. We need to make a lot of women understand they are really feminists before this is going to happen.

"In the mid-1970s feminism was considered largely a white middle-class movement. The public perception of feminists has narrowed much farther in the mid-1980s. Now most young professional women claim no tie to feminism—because feminists have been identified with the radical fringe, the militant lesbian separatists such as Robin Morgan, who never seems to shut up. Too many straight women have just dropped out of the movement.

"All women need to understand economic issues are their issues, whether they're married or single, working or not, mothers or childless. Apparently, we need to make the gender gap wider. Too many of us went along with the 66 percent of white males who vote for Reagan."

As long as the average woman is poorer than the average man, such an animal as women's economic issues exists. Any woman whose financial security depends on finding a husband or keeping the one she's got has no security. "Yet too few women understand these facts or perceive them as a call to action," Sheron says. "You might as well tell women to masturbate."

Kara, who recognizes and resents the status quo, says pessimistically, "It's not going to change. *Maybe* it could change if women got very mad again, only mad in a more positive way.

"I'm not so sure getting mad at men personally will accomplish anything. That personal anger is too hard to sustain. We really can't do without them, can we? So how can we stay furiously mad at them?

"We would have to get mad about hard economic issues and fight them one by one. But we would have to do this without becoming hysterical around men. Women cry when they get mad. I can't even argue with my brother without crying if I'm really hurt by what he says."

Again and again when we talk about money, about workplace issues, we talk about the difficulty we have in separating the personal from the professional. "Women often avoid conflict in the workplace," Sheron says, "because they can't be angry without being emotional. Yet avoiding conflict keeps them down. And now there is another problem: Women identify anger with feminism, with harshness, with being unfeminine. A lot of these women tell you they're playing the 'game' when actually they are being nonassertive."

The rhetoric of the women's movement turned off a lot of women who might have become politically active, who might be working even now to win true pay equality for women. "Basically most women do believe what the movement is saying: equal rights for women. But a lot of them don't know they believe it because of the way the spokeswomen presented the message," Sheron says.

Excesses of rhetoric left ordinary women feeling outside a movement that could and should be helping them get to where they are going now. In the Midwest, we seldom felt "they" were speaking *to* us. And surely they were not speaking *for* us, though they should have been. Far more women live in the rest of the country than reside in New York City or Los Angeles.

Sometimes our spokeswomen seemed to have absolutely no notion of who we were and what our lives were like. In her nonsexist child-rearing guide, *Growing up Free,* Letty Cottin Pogrebin told us that our children would forsake the sexist lyrics of the Rolling Stones for the more acceptable words of gay feminist folk singer Holly Near. I remember reading that and laughing: *I* would not trade Mick Jagger and the Stones, no matter how sexist, for Near. So why should my son?

In those days feminists debated Phyllis Schlafly about whether or not the ERA would lead to coed bathrooms. Too many of us got the impression the women's movement was more concerned about who opened our car doors and did our dishes than salaries. The movement put a lot of energy into defending a lesbian's right to sleep with another woman—when they should have focused on her right to work. We antagonized Middle America for no good reason. We did not change its mind about homosexuality.

The excesses were necessary in the very beginning, as they are in any movement, to galvanize a following, to attract attention to a just cause. They haven't been necessary for a long time, yet some movement leaders are still mired in their own excesses of ideology whereas others, notably Friedan, have had little success in their attempts to provide us with a second stage.

They haven't given ordinary women a bridge from then to now. Women, especially single women, are in transition. We are no longer fashionable, yet our demographics promise that we will be someday again. Unmarried baby-boom women will soon be regarded as a target audience for advertisers who have realized the odds are we never will wed. It would be nice if we drew the conclusion first, if we began making our life plans before marketing men made them for us.

"I think I know where women should be," Jillian says, "but I'm not exactly sure how we should get there. I am convinced getting there begins in a very personal way, with each woman saying, 'There probably is no man out there for me. I probably will never marry. And that's okay.'

"From the very personal we will need to move to the political to change entirely the way people are paid for the work they do. This time around I think we should leave homosexuality and housework out of it. This time the subject is money."

It all comes down to that—money; but also sex, personal and political issues, and choices. Can we turn them from problems to solutions?

Carolyn insists we can't. "We are misled by the women's movement," she says. "They never told us the truth about working, about anything."

When I met Carolyn, she asked if she would be paid for giving me an interview on my topic, how the threat of nuclear war affects children. Lawrence, Kansas, Carolyn's home, was the site of ABC's television movie "The Day After"; and I was in Lawrence talking to Carolyn at the same time other journalists were converging on the town asking residents what it felt like to be blown away on TV. I wasn't surprised that she expected to be paid.

But she apologized: "I'm so money obsessed."

She told me her story about child-support checks that were inadequate and usually late, a salary barely above minimum wage, her running battles with utility companies and overdrawn checking accounts, a familiar story to anyone who writes about women. The answers to these women's problems aren't easy ones. Yet I always find myself trying to provide answers over coffee or glasses of white wine, out of guilt because I should be giving something back in exchange for their stories, out of love because all women's stories are so much alike, so much like my own.

I asked her if she knew anything about comparable pay; and she didn't. Retail sales clerks are part of the vast pink-collar ghetto, I said, women whose services are valued less by society than those of blue-collar workers, largely men.

She said, "There is nothing *I* can do about that. I'm stuck."

I thought about something Christine often says: "If you think you're trapped in a job with no future, if you think you have no career options, you focus on the personal aspect of your life as the way out of the trap. A single woman on a career track doesn't need a man for the same reasons a secretary does. Her focus is different. It isn't fair, but it's true."

Carolyn would agree with Christine's analysis; and she identifies herself as one of the trapped. If you think you're trapped, you are.

I asked if she would consider joining a union of sales clerks (should one exist), if she would commit herself to a political movement that promised to achieve pay equity for her. And she said, "No, I am not a libber."

Then we talked about kids and the bomb, a topic about which she feels strongly. Carolyn is very antinuke. (In 1984, she assured me, "Reagan would never start a nuclear war; and he won't raise taxes either.") But we got back to money.

I suggested she see an attorney and ask about having her child support reviewed by the court. She said she couldn't afford an attorney. I suggested legal aid, a store-front law clinic, a women's center. "Call your local NOW chapter for advice," I said. She said, "Well . . ."

Could she let her ex-husband play a greater role in the children's lives? I asked. Would he not buy the sneakers or book bags or whatever if he saw them enough to treat them in the natural way fathers treat children—which includes buying what they need as a matter of course?

She said he had "forfeited" his rights.

So we drank more coffee; and she asked me about my life. I told her I'd had joint custody of my only child since our divorce, when he was eight. She said, "How does that work?"

After we got the logistics down, very well.

"But doesn't having two homes confuse your son?" she asked. "Shouldn't children be with their mother?"

In the beginning, having two homes did confuse him. And obviously shared custody is not perfect. A solid marriage between two loving people who will never make mistakes as spouses or parents is ideal, but it was not one of the choices we had. We went for the strong second. Shared custody has required understanding and maturity of all of us, including my son's stepmother. We have made it work; and I do not think we are extraordinary people.

And yes, children belong with their mother, and also with their father—fathers and mothers being the two people who will love their children best.

Carolyn was polite, but she didn't agree. She disapproved. I was used to getting that reaction, especially from women, divorced mothers who needed to believe what they were doing was right.

Ten years ago women were complaining that men did not share the housework, the child care. And thousands of fathers began sharing the child care. We called them "new fathers," a breed who, if not exactly equal partners in the dirty diaper department, were more involved than their fathers or our fathers had been.

Then we divorced them. And we became traditional ex-wives complaining because the support checks were too small, too late. We held these new fathers to the visitation rights prescribed by law. Our neighbors, friends, and relatives could call and say, "Can I take the child out for a pizza?" and get a positive response from us, but their fathers couldn't. And we began a quest called "finding a new daddy" for the children.

EXCELLENT QUESTION) Why have we discarded all those reasonably good daddys because our marriages to them didn't work out?

Carolyn insists *her* former husband is not a good father. Maybe he isn't a good father anymore. Or maybe he never was. An outsider cannot judge the quality of an absent father's care. But so many women make the same negative comment about the men they considered suitable fathers at the time of conception.

Until recently expert opinion on joint custody was split. The weight of opinion is beginning to shift to the pro position. And lawyers tell me joint-custody mothers do receive child support when they earn less than fathers—and joint-custody fathers are more likely to pay than noncustodial fathers.

"Joint custody won't catch on," Carolyn said. "Because all women have is our children. We aren't going to give up *that*."

"That" is power, maternal power, the only power a woman in reduced economic circumstances, a woman left poorer by divorce, feels she has. That sense of power is false.

Carolyn insisted, "It just can't work for everyone. You are special. You lead an exotic life."

Well, Jillian and I laughed about that later. We agreed my life is as exotic as an Illinois field in late August, overgrown with black-eyed Susan, pampas grass, goldenrod. I mailed Carolyn a package of books and articles on shared custody, comparable worth, careers for women. She sent me a thank-you note illustrated by two kittens, a ball of yarn, a basket of daisies.

Carolyn rejected what I offered as potential solutions because they were too personal—suited only for me—and too political, requiring a level of organizational involvement she rejected. She was, she said, trapped. The only way out was marriage. She still believed in the agreement.

"Too many of us still don't know where to put our trust except in men," Jilllan says. "Where else do we put it? We've not had a history of trusting each other. I have a friend who works in an office where the administrative assistant, a woman, spies on the other women employees for her boss. She's like the 'Liz' character in the movie *9 to 5*.

"There are still enough women out there like her, women who need male approval so badly they will sell the rest of us out—enough of them to provide ample excuses for the women who don't want to trust their own sex anyway."

But Christine insists, "Women who sell other women out are beginning to lose face. We are expecting more of each other. On a personal level, we really need each other.

"I can't stand those women who drop their friends when they start dating a man. In my group, we don't do that. We invite everyone over for drinks to meet him. Sometimes, of course, he does get interested in a woman he meets through one of us. So what?

"My friends are very important to me, more important than a date. They will be my friends for life. When single people say they are lonely, they are missing that sense of family they had when they were growing up. They want to create the continuity, the shared history, that marriage provides.

"We are all trying to weave a tapestry of our lives. Family and friends are the recurring threads of our tapestries. Men come and go. They are like broken threads; and it's disconcerting to have those broken threads, so you want to find a man who will stay, one you can weave into the fabric.

"Women forget you can also weave in those broken threads and have a beautiful, very original tapestry design—if you also have the strong constant threads of family and friends. I wouldn't sacrifice my friends for a man.

"Almost everybody I know now would like to be married. They want to share their lives, not find someone to make their lives, to make them happy. If you can't be happy alone, you can't be happy with someone. I think it's a terrible shame when women say they are waiting to find someone, waiting to be happy.

"No one should ever wait to be happy."

When I was unhappily married, I was waiting to be happy. I remember waking up some mornings with a sense of expectation, then realizing everything was the same; and the expectations went flat. I have to concentrate to conjure those feelings now it's been so long since I had anything like them.

I am certainly not the person I was when I walked out on my marriage, when I chose to be single, in 1976. She was a child-woman. She might never have become an adult if she had remained wrapped in the cocoon woven by her indulgent husband. I am an independent, interesting woman, a survivor. Like Jenny, I am good company. My life is very much what I thought it should be when I left.

As a wife, I existed in a world peopled by white Catholic mothers and lots of little white Catholic children. We shuffled back and forth between each other's houses, school, church, shopping malls, soccer fields, like plastic play family people all painted the same color.

Now I live in an integrated neighborhood; and my friends are men, women, Jews, WASPs, Catholics, straights, gays. I have many close women friends, almost sisters, who can always be counted on, will surely understand. My work is interesting; and I have been lucky with men. They have given me orgasms and laughs, friendship and love, insights into the human condition I couldn't have gotten from women. I have never had a bad lover. Some were merely adequate, yes; but never bad

Most important, ours was a victimless divorce.

Richard and I have stood by each other as coparents for half of our son's life. Like the friendly diplomats of two countries, we have little in common except goodwill. He is happier in his second marriage to a woman who shares his faith, his politics and habits.

And my son, Richard, is a person I like and enjoy, apart from the pride I have in being his mother. He told me not long ago that he is proud of me too—"because you have guts, Mother."

I don't think this is something he would have been able to say had his mother remained in that marriage.

I am not sure exactly where I am going, but I do know how to get there: with the encouragement and support of other women, on the strength of my own desires, abilities, talents, *guts*, not a man's. No, I don't think I'll ever marry again. I do not think there is a man "out there" for me. And really it does not matter. That choice may not be mine to make, but all the other choices are.

35 APPEAL OF YOUNG
42
43